MAN WITH
A WOMB

ALSO BY L.A. JOHNTRE

JohnTre's Guide to Sexuality & Acceptance in the U.S.
March 2007

MAN WITH
A WOMB

By L.A. JohnTre

L. Johnverrell

ISBN – 978-1-4303-1689-3

The JohnTre Corporation

L.A. JohnTre

~~JohnTre, L.A.~~   Johnverrell, L.

   Man With A Womb / by L Johnverrell – 4th U.S. ed.

ISBN – 978-1-4303-1689-3

~~For "Vee" and "Tee", my only reasons for still breathing.~~

This book is still for "Vee" and "Tee", of course, but I have found other reasons why I have to keep breathing. ☺

Note: The first version of this book was written in 2006. I have added a few pages and changed a few items, due to changes in my life and personality as of 2010. I hope you enjoy reading where I've been, and my mindset now.

MAN WITH A WOMB

December 2, 2006
10:58 AM
Lithonia, GA USA
(Location: by the lake)

I love these apartments. Well maybe not love them, but I like them a lot. I chose them because they have a lake with a fountain that shoots water in the center. I'm thankful that they allowed me to move in when no one else would. Let's just say that I'm blackballed from the Atlanta apartment community!

I'm very hurt right now. I'm holding back some tears. Someone that I was dating is not as interested in me as I had hoped she was. In case the cover fooled you, or if you just didn't know, I am a lesbian. I am a female that has romantic interest in only other females. You may have thought I was a man. Don't feel embarrassed. It happens all the time. That said, I think I will answer the biggest stereotypical question that faces lesbians like me on the very first page of my book. "Do I think that I am a man?" The answer is yes *and* no.

I *am* a man. I just happen to have a *womb* for child bearing. I know that I am still a woman, and quite happy about it!

I guess that makes *all* women, *men with wombs*. True. Actually, that definition was given to me by a MARTA* train preacher. They are very popular here in Atlanta. Someone will just sit by you on the commuter train and start telling you the Word of God the way he or she sees it. They get an entire 60-seat congregation for less than two dollars fare! He told me that a woman is just an extension of a man and existed only for childbirth and a man's pleasure. Amazing as how as much of a sexist view he had for a woman's purpose on this Earth, he couldn't have given me a better phrase to describe myself!

I've done my child bearing duty, as he put it. I have two pre-teen daughters that I am raising with the help of their fathers. I don't ever see myself in a heterosexual relationship again. I have loved women ever since my first crush in the fifth grade.

Like most gay youth, I denied who I was, and hoped that my desire for women would go away simply because I was afraid. I was always a tomboy, but not the average one. I didn't climb trees or anything like that, but I loved boy's toys and clothing! I never wanted to dress like a girl. I hated wearing girl's clothing with extreme passion and it would follow me into adulthood, as would my love for women. I love to see a feminine woman shop, dress and put on makeup. The feminine qualities that I lack and do not desire to have are the very ones that intrigue me most in a woman.

I didn't come out until I was twenty four years old. I had no idea what I would encounter being a dominant butch lesbian! There is not only the animosity that exists for lesbians like me in heterosexuals, but also within the gay and lesbian community! There is hate, within a hate, *within* a hate that most do not understand or even know exists!

I'm taking deep breaths as I write because I know that I am about to relive some devastating moments of my past with you. It is something that must be done. After 36 years. it's time for me to move on. I think that everyone should tell their story and put their past in writing. It's like closing up, saving a file and giving you a chance for a fresh start. I chose this time because it is the most painful. It is strange, but I can only do my best when I am in so much pain.

Don't get me wrong. It's not all about this particular woman. I've only known her a few weeks, but everyone that I allow into my personal space leaves a mark in my heart. I know now that it is best to keep your personal space small, especially if people don't understand who you are, and why you do the things you do.

Why do I dress only in men's clothing? Why does only the most feminine and motherly qualities in a woman interest me? Why do I take interests in rainbows, nature and animals? Why do I not believe that I can find true love? Why did I pick a cold December day to sit in front of a lake and write?

Pain is cold. Life is cold. I am in pain, sitting in the cold and writing about my life! It's perfect!

The lake, the trees, and the squirrels are keeping me company so much that I think they deserve the first copy of this book. I will come down to the edge of the lake and sink it when it comes off the press. *I like doing ceremonial stuff like that.*

Will it wash away my past and the pain? Probably not. It will just turn into a soggy book at the bottom of an apartment lake! But, it will mean something to me. It would save and close a file.

I am not a writer, so there are no fancy words in this book. I must tell you this as if you were sitting on this bench freezing along with me. Someone once told me that I am a starter and not a finisher, so I pray that the pain I feel when writing this is strong enough for me to finish. Have you ever heard someone pray for pain? I do. It helps me finish things. Perhaps I should find another incentive, but for now, it will have to do.

-L.A. JohnTre

*MARTA - Metropolitan Atlanta Rapid Transit Authority.

December 9, 2006
3:00 PM
Lithonia, Georgia USA
(Location: by the lake, *again*)

It's *really* cold this time by the lake! It's so cold that the fountain that shoots up water has frozen solid! It fits because I'm frozen, too! It is a week later and its official. The woman that I was interested in has totally closed the door on me. What I don't understand is that a few days ago right after I wrote that first entry, she invited me to her house and we made love. *(At least that is what I was doing!)*

I really liked this young woman. She is still in her twenties, an artist from Germany, and quite beautiful. Ok. Yes, I am a sucker for a woman that speaks another language, and that adores the arts! That is what captivated me about her in the first place. Today, it became evident, that she wasn't meant for me, but someone else.

That is really putting the situation lightly because I am hurting like hell right now! But, that's good because I'm in pain enough to write! Maybe I'm just too old for the dating game. I have an old briefcase in my closet with hotel keys and letters from those days. *(You'll hear about them later)* I'm back to the old fashioned way of thinking that when a woman invites you, whether you are a man or a woman, into her home and you are intimate, that means that she wants a relationship with you! Right! *Right?* That's not necessarily so!

When I asked her if she wanted to be my girlfriend afterwards, she said that it was too soon. *Too soon?* She said that she didn't know me well enough to know if she wanted to get that serious with me! Then, she took another puff of her cigarette. Wow! I felt like such a chump. I really liked this woman, but I was just a booty call. I think I was a replacement booty call at that! I think she wanted someone else to come, but I ended up being the one that showed up!

I told my daughters that I would be fine. I don't take rejection well at all. I have very unhealthy crying outbursts and have to get some air. I'm beginning to also understand why some people choose to become a recluse.

My self diagnosis? I'm just really depressed. Am I Bipolar? No, I don't have any suicidal intentions anymore. In fact, I want to show the world that I can survive it! If I have to find solitude writing in the cold beside a freezing apartment lake, then so be it! The choice is mine! I can either take prescription medication subscribed by a licensed professional, or write my story and drop my past into a lake for closure! *(If my choice doesn't work, I promise to try the therapy and medication)*

I think that before you read about someone's past, then you should know what is happening with that person at the time he or she is writing. I'm writing these journal-like passages just for that purpose. You see that I am hurt because of another failed attempt at starting a relationship with someone. I have also deemed this as the last time *I* will pursue a potential mate! From now on, I will just wait until true love finds me.

What is my definition of true love? That would take another book, but the short answer is to have someone that loves you at the same time you love them! I have never experienced that. Most of us are caught up in that "I love you more", or "you love me more" situation on either side of the table. That's lopsided love!

Are you familiar with Monique's character on *The Parkers* television show? She loves the professor, but the professor doesn't love her, and she makes a total fool of herself every episode! Yes, that has been me on both ends, and I don't want to be a lopsided lover, or have someone lopping me anymore, either! I want someone that wants me, and that I truly want her.

So from now on, I'm just waiting for her to show up! I have a feeling that it's going to take a while, too!

On wanting a family? Well, I really don't have a family besides my daughters, my ex-husband and two older brothers. That's something that I've always desired. I usually end up borrowing my mate's families and when the mate leaves, so does the family!

The memories of sitting around a table and eating Thanksgiving and Christmas dinners are long gone. I've never dressed a full family dinner table for myself and the people I love because—well, there haven't been enough people around to love!

My search for love and a family has caused me the greatest amount of pain.

-L.A. JohnTre

Chapter 1

Mary Had Her Little Lamb

They say you aren't a true Atlantan unless you are a Grady Baby. Well, I am as true as they come, because I was born in August of 1970 at Henry Grady Memorial Hospital in Atlanta, Georgia. I was one month premature at four measly pounds and seven ounces with a fever of one hundred and three degrees! I've heard the story a million times how the doctors took me from my mother and dumped me in a huge bucket of ice to get my fever down.

My mother, Mary, was thirty-seven years old and threatening miscarriage throughout her pregnancy with me, as she did with the three stillbirths before me. My mother prayed for a girl. She had two boys already and wanted a girl! She even told the doctor to do whatever he could to save me because having a daughter meant everything to her! Sure enough, those Grady doctors got my fever down and I was released a week after my mother. She named me "Lisa", after her favorite character on the daytime soap opera, *Guiding Light*.

My parents, brothers and grandmother lived off Simpson Road in Atlanta, when I was born. My father's name is Nathaniel. At my time of birth, he was a brick mason for his uncle's construction company in Macon, Georgia. Well, at least that what it says on my birth certificate. I never really knew the guy! According to my mother, he was primarily a street hustler. I have never met my father's side of the family, but I hear that most of them still reside in Macon.

My parents broke up long before I started school. I was just a newborn when a Black man with a beard and blue cap robbed the C&S Bank downtown. My mother and grandmother were watching the news when the Blue Cap Bank Robber was pictured leaving the scene of the crime with over $8,000! They knew who it was immediately!

That night they did not even open the door for my father and he had to break a window to get into the house. He poured the money out of his bag all over the bed where I was laying. My grandmother said that I was just crumpling up hundred dollar bills and gurgling! They had a huge argument over the bank robbery. My mother told him to leave and to take the money with him! He left a few hundred dollars on the bed for me and my brothers and fled. They never caught him or recovered the money.

My mother moved us away from Simpson Road to the West End area. I would spend most of my childhood there. Mom was overly protective of me because of my asthma and heart conditions. I could not go outside to play even in the summer time! I was her little princess. I was always in the house and doing something for her or my grandmother. When I was not doing something for them, I was bothering my older brothers, Perry and Tim. They were twelve and thirteen years older than I was, and since I was the only girl and the youngest, I was a spoiled, rotten brat of a little sister. Tim would buy me my Christmas gifts every year after he got his first job, and Perry would sneak me candy and money whenever he could!

My mother never let me go with my dad to meet his family in Macon because she said that he only wanted to take me and never invited her. By the mid seventies, they hardly spoke, and the only information I would have is that I have two fraternal brothers and another sister somewhere. It never bothered me because I had my mom, my grandmother, my brothers and a whole bunch of people that would come to my mom's house every day. They were my family.

My mother had many friends in the early days. She was a Head Mother of Father Abraham's Church congregation on Ira Street in the seventies. Father Abraham was like Atlanta's local version of Reverend Ike. He always prophesied the three-digit blessing. It came out every day around five o'clock from Wall Street in New York City. The illegal lottery number was the first digit of the morning closing volume of the Dow Jones, and the last two from the closing bell. *It was how the stock market mattered in the hood!*

My mother was referred to as "Lady Natural", in the church, and simply by her middle name, Hellen, in the numbers game. Our house was one of the key links from Atlanta to New York City. People would go through our back yard, write their daily selection on tiny slips of paper, and drop them in the empty birdbath throughout the day. When they would "hit", they would come over and buy my mother a fifth of Seagram's gin and collect their winnings. She would get her commission, and then we would have a party! I would be the chosen disc jockey for the night.

Bible study, wig shows and tea parties would be almost every day for our house. We were conveniently located next to Mr. Skeeters on Lucille Ave in the West End. He was the liquor man. The routine was to grab your liquor at Mr. Skeeters, go next door to Hellen's house to drink, play your numbers for the next day, and even gamble if it was Po-Ke-No night! My mother did not associate with much of her biological family, but she found one of her own with the church folks and hoodlums of Atlanta in the seventies and early eighties. You couldn't tell who was who either. Everyone was an equal at Hellen's house!

She was highly loved and well known. If someone called Atlanta Police about the noise, she knew almost everyone on the police force, including Commissioners Eaves and Brown. The officers would just come in and have some of my grandmother's cooking before getting back into their patrol cars and leaving.

I got my business sense from my mother as well. She only worked briefly as a house cleaner in Lynwood Park, as did my grandmother, for the Schledenhaffen family. They were very nice people and offered my mother work whenever she needed extra money. It was the only legitimate job that she would have in her life. Although my mother and grandmother were born in Elberton, Georgia, they called Lynwood Park in Buckhead home for many years.

Mom stopped working and started her first company, Mary's Wig Fair, in the late seventies. I remember her taking that business all the way to doing a fashion show at the Peachtree Plaza Hotel. In addition to the parties, housekeeping and the racketeering, my mother would style hair for the many clients that came to our house. I would always get to play with the customer's children and that was a relief! They were so many grown people in the house all of the time that I would always enjoy company that was my age. Since my mother had both legitimate and illegal businesses, there was a variety of people coming to the house.

There was so much entertaining to do that my mother hired her friend, Georgia, to be our house cleaner. I was being waited on hand and foot! I had my mom, grandmother *and* a maid to fix my meals and clean my room.

Mom also had borders stay in our extra bedrooms from time to time. Some people say that I have a Northern accent when I speak. I always say that it may be because of the diversity of the borders that stayed with my family! I used to have dinner with people that spoke many different languages beside English. I also heard many stories!

It was fun for me to sit at the dinner table and hear about how Reverend Bell was at the March on Washington, or how Mr. Moko, one of the best bounty hunters in Georgia, was shot three times and still brought the guy to jail! Once, there was even a man from Brooklyn that fought the Son of Sam killer away from his girlfriend! *Well, at least that is what he said he did!* I will always remember those great dinner table moments!

We didn't have to worry about money often, because my mother usually kept a lot of it. She always bought me the best in little girls clothing that I never liked. I remember those dressy leather shoes and those white stockings with the lace. *Yuck!* I really hated those! That seemed to be the criteria for my Easter dress every year.

I remember going with her to Kesslers downtown to shop and being in the little girls section. I always wanted to go downstairs to the boy's section, near the Men's Den to pick out a something to wear. I would never tell my mother that! It would be asking for a slap in the face! When I used to pick out my clothes, she would be the first to say that little girls didn't wear that! She purchased a lot of dresses and jumpsuits for me to start school in every year.

I went to Mary Agnes Jones Elementary school in Atlanta. That was back when they had an older building and elementary schools gone up to the seventh grade! I cannot remember my first grade teacher's name because I could never pronounce it correctly. *She used to paddle us just for that! Boy, school times have really changed!*

I would learn where my biggest focus of ridicule attack would come from that first day around lunchtime. As we formed the line for the bell, I stood next to Eldridge, who would be my first bully, and asked him what our teacher said about something in class. I do not even remember the questions, but he answered every one of them with either, "No, Big Lips!", or "Yes, Big Lips!"

I have big lips! I found out that day in the first grade that I had a defect. What was the big deal about me having big lips? Anyway, I would be teased almost every day of my grade school years about the big lips, or the fact that I walked on my tiptoes. Both of these traits inherited from Nathaniel. Gee, thanks dad! Well, at least he gave me something!

Yes, that's me in 1978.

Chapter 2

Grade School Combatant

What do I remember most about my grade school days? I don't remember as much of the learning part as I do the fights and ridicule! I was dubbed a tomboy in the first grade almost instantly. The boys always wanted to fight me because I was so big and boy-like. I wasn't a bully, but I was really large for my age. My first battle would be with Eldridge. This boy just did not like me for some reason! We got into a fight by the flagpole after school. I should not say it was a fight because that would mean that I would have to at least gotten one lick in! I didn't. He punched me one time and I walked away holding my face. I didn't cry afterwards and I think that made him very angry. He said that he would beat me up again the next day.

When I got home after the altercation with Eldridge, my mother was preparing to go to the hospital. She was about to have what would be the first of many operations. She was scheduled to have a tumor removed in her left breast. Well, at least that is what she thought. The cancer had spread and doctors had to remove her left breast entirely, as well as most of her underarm. She was told that she would never lift that arm again and could never have vitals taken from it. Mom spent days in Crawford Long Hospital and received flowers and cards from visitors. Her guestbook noted that over 250 people came to see her. I rode with her when she finally came home. I never told her about the fight with Eldridge at school, but she found out about it soon enough!

While my mother was in the hospital, I had taken care of my problem with Eldridge and the other boys bullying me. Perry had a gun hidden under his bed and I knew about it. I didn't know that it wasn't loaded. I didn't even know how to use it, but I took it to school, and warned Eldridge and the other boys not to pick on me ever again. They didn't!

The gun incident was not even mentioned until some weeks later. I got mad at my teacher and a student yelled out, "Don't make her mad, she'll bring that gun again!" The principal called my mother, who had been home resting, and had a conference with her. I wasn't suspended from school since no one was hurt in the incident, and they could never prove that I brought the gun to school in the first place! I wasn't confessing to anything! I had already returned the gun to my brother's dresser. I watched just as many cop television shows back then as I do now, and even at eight years old, I knew how to wipe it down for fingerprints before I put it back! I only showed it to the boys that were bullying me, and they were all too scared to talk up for the one student that tattled on me in class! It was peaceful for five grades after that.

I rescued my first damsel in distress in the fifth grade. She would be my first crush. Tracy was the prettiest girl in class, and the boys were always trying to get her to "go with them" or "give them a chance," as we used to say. One of the girls thought that Tracy had kissed her boyfriend and was about to slap her when I intervened. The boys were even still afraid of me, so when I jumped in between the girl and Tracy, she backed off quickly due to my reputation!

Tracy never had a boyfriend. She always hung around me and I was fine with that. It got to the point where my former bullies were trying to be my best friend just to get to her! She probably didn't like boys because she had problems at home. Her father was always abusing her mother, and she shared this with me only with the promise that I would not tell anyone. I kept my promise and never did, just so she would stay my friend. When her mother finally got tired of the abuse, they left her father and moved back home to Ohio. I was upset to lose my first crush, but glad that they were escaping that situation.

On her last day, Tracy and I said our goodbyes and hugged. As we pulled away, I kissed her on the lips. I couldn't tell you why I did it. It just felt like it was right. She looked at me for a moment and smiled. Just before she ran away, she opened her shirt, flashed me her little boobs, and stuck her tongue out! I was only ten years old but was even serious back then. I kiss you and you show me your mini breasts and run? I wanted her to kiss me back, but all I got was a tease. *It was a sign of times to come, perhaps.*

I remember coming home from school one day and seeing some very tall men in suits at our house. They were different from mom's usual guests because they weren't friendly at all. One of them stood very closely behind my mother and had his jacket around her shoulders. These men were from New York, and evidently, my mother was not reporting her profits in the numbers game as she was supposed to do!

I found out much later in life that the man standing behind her had a gun to her back and that they had threatened to kill my brothers and me if my mother did not close her numbers operation. Of course, she stopped to protect us and the change hit us hard financially and emotionally.

After my mother stopped racketeering in the early eighties, her health began to worsen, and her friend count started to become smaller. It appears that most of them were around for just the parties that we could no longer afford. We had to move to another house on Avon Avenue, and I changed schools. This house was much smaller and we needed all the rooms for ourselves and could not take in borders.

Mom was so broke when we first moved in that we could not turn on our electricity. At first, Tim would rig the light meter box with a clothes hanger to turn the power on. Georgia Power quickly caught on to that and took our meter away! Then, we ran an extension cord to my neighbor's house for just enough power to run one television and a crock dish to cook. I remember watching the news when President Reagan was shot on that small black and white television set in the middle of our kitchen. In fact, the news was all I remembered watching on that set! We didn't have a cord long enough to reach into my room to power mine, so I had to watch whatever my mother watched.

My mom was reading in the summer of 1981 when she heard some crashing noises in the living room. My grandmother was staying with a friend while our power was off, and we would be glad she was. Kerosene lamps were lighting our living room and one of them had exploded unto a sofa. Our entire living room was in flames. My mother panicked, woke up Perry from his bedroom, and they quickly rushed outside of the burning house.

It was about ten seconds after they got outside when they remembered that I was still in the house sleeping! Perry rushed backed into the house and woke me up. Because I was sleepy, I was fighting him and trying to get back into the bed! I did not know the house was on fire, of course! He tossed me out of an open window and then jumped himself.

Perry saved my life. He never talks about it, but he did. The firefighters didn't arrive until almost an hour after he rescued me. I had heard firefighters that visited our school say that you are never supposed to go back into a burning house—but my brother did just that! If he hadn't disobeyed the rule, I'd be dead now! I always get choked up just thinking about it.

My mom did not have renters insurance. A lot of the stuff that she had bought from her racketeering days was destroyed; including a $400 velvet canvass oil painting, a dining room armoire full of crystal, and a genuine leather bar and stool set! It all went up in smoke! My mom would later say that it was the Lord's way of preparing her to live a more honest life.

After the Avon house fire, the Red Cross found us a house on Westlake Avenue, and again—I changed schools. In November of that same year, my then 71-year old grandmother passed away in her sleep. We had twin beds and slept in the same room, so I saw her when I left that morning.

My grandmother, Lizzie, was always rescuing me from my mom's few punishments. She was affectionately known as Grandmother Stringbean throughout Lynwood Park and Elberton for many years. She would be the last smoker in our immediate family, and her favorites were Kent cigarettes and Schlitz beer.

If you gave her some beer and cigarettes, she would shut up in her room the rest of the night watching television!

My mother took my grandmother's death very hard. She kept me out of school a whole month just so that she can have me at the house. Her funeral was extremely emotional. A lot of crying and even Perry and Tim were overcome with grief. It would be the only time in my life that I would ever see both of them cry.

I was absent from school so much after that, I was refrained one grade. My test scores were great, and I was on level, but the school would not pass me based on attendance. My mother kept me out of school a lot, even before my grandmother passed away. All I had to do was say that I just did not want to go! She really wanted me at home to be her little girl.

My mom began to focus on her wig business again after my grandmother's passing. I focused on packing. I knew that she would not be able to stay in the house where she died for very long, so I got a head start on preparing for the next place. I also didn't want to repeat the sixth grade in the same school that kept me back, so I was ready to move this time. We rented an apartment on Newport Street, so that we could be closer to one of my mom's best friends, Mrs. Derrico. The Derrico's were like family to us and my mom had known her for many years. They had attended Father Abraham's Church together and were both head mothers. She was one of the few friends that did not abandon my mother after she stopped racketeering, and even sung at my grandmother's funeral.

There was one problem about that move. My new school would be John F. Kennedy Middle. At that time, Kennedy was one of the roughest schools in the city. My pistol packing reputation from M. Agnes Jones was long gone. I would be on my own here. It only took a few days before I was being called "big lipped and tip toed" again. I got into three fights with boys my first week. I wasn't much of a fighter, and the boys that I had to fight were huge! It got to the point where I just did not fight back, and took the ridicule. It would be a long sixth grade repeat!

I made it through most of the first months after the holiday break without another fight until two boys cornered me in the parking lot while walking home. I began to walk faster, but they wouldn't leave me alone. It was the "big lips" thing again! I ran down Newport Street with tears in my eyes, dropping my books and papers everywhere! Suddenly, I looked up and saw Perry and Tim running after the boys followed by one of Mrs. Derrico's sons!

They caught up with them and made them pick up my dropped papers and apologize. Now, they were the one's crying! The rest of the time at Kennedy was peaceful because news of my brothers spread throughout the school. Don't pick on her or she will send her brothers on you they'd say! She has about six of them and they are huge! They must have been counting Mrs. Derrico's sons as my brothers too! *I never bothered to clear that up with them either!*

It seemed like every time I got the bullying situation under control I had to change schools again. Mom had to turn to government housing assistance and I had to transfer in the middle of the school year. This would be my third school in the sixth grade!

We moved to Lawton Street in a duplex. It was now just my mom and me. My brothers had children and moved into their own places with their girlfriends after we moved from the house where my grandmother died. I would finally have my own room, but I was still troubled. Moving to Lawton Street meant that I was going right back where I started at M. Agnes Jones—this time one year behind my original class who were seventh graders now!

My first day back, in the cafeteria, I saw my now seventh grade original classmates. Which one recognized me first? Eldridge! He was bigger now and obviously a better kid. He just said that he remembered me and patted me on the back. None of them even asked me why I was kept back a grade. They were just glad to see me back. I was shocked, and relieved.

My desire to be with girls came into play more than anything that sixth grade year. I was simply, totally, outrageously crushing over three girls in my class! I couldn't get very close to them like I did Tracy however. Something else had happened to me in the school ranks. I had become the smart nerd of the class! It is not surprising. After all, I was only repeating the sixth grade because of an attendance refrain at another school, not because I didn't know the work. Since I was a nerd now, I couldn't even get to be friends with the popular girls that I liked. My last two grade school years were a piece of cake. I didn't have to worry about the bullying because it seemed the kids had matured at that school.

Now, I had to deal with the fact that my attraction for girls was becoming stronger as I was moving into my high school years.

Chapter 3

Vincit Qui Se Vincit

"He conquers who conquers himself." That is the school motto, (spoken in English), for the historic institution on 45 Whitehouse Drive in Atlanta, Georgia!

It was just like in the film, *Rudy*, where the kid only wanted to go to Notre Dame his whole life and play football for the Irish. He had watched Notre Dame Football with his father and family and always said that he was going to go to that school and play football. He did! Now, it was not as challenging to get into Booker T. Washington High School as it is Notre Dame, but the way I was carrying on about finally going to this school—you would think it was!

My brothers, the Derrico kids, local "Stomp, Jump and Twist" celebrity disc jockey Ed "Mojo" Lyons, Lena Horne *and* Dr. Martin Luther King, Jr. all went to Washington High School! I wanted to go and leave a legacy on those blue and white halls! Well, at least they *used* to be blue and white. My eighth grade class just happened to arrive during a renovation in 1984 when they were then painted a dull, hospital beige-like disaster!

Like all kids that are pumped up about getting to walk the halls of high school, I had a quick reality check. It came in the form of an egg being tossed at me from a fourth floor window! It was while in the girl's bathroom washing the egg off my jacket that I thought that maybe this wasn't going to be all that I had expected.

Everyone knew Perry from his days at Washington, from my homeroom teacher Mr. Suleiman, to Principal Collins himself! My brother had left me some big shoes to fill, and I had no idea how important it would be to him for me to be popular like he was! He was platoon leader for the entire JROTC department and wanted me to get in good with the now late Sgt. Allen, who was his mentor. Unfortunately for him, I would never be offered the opportunity to join JROTC. I was relieved by that, myself!

I had my own dilemmas to deal with. This was high school! In elementary school when a girl dresses and runs like a boy, she can be simply labeled as a tomboy. No biggie! It is just a phase for her that she will grow out of by the age of thirteen, and she will be ready to gossip with her friends, and talk about boys and makeup! I was fourteen with tall boys everywhere with mustaches and muscles, but all I could think about is that one girl that sat across from me in English class with those pretty eyes!

I could not hide it at this age. I wasn't girly-girly at all! By the second day of high school classes, I was called a "bulldagger" by one of the upperclassmen. That is mostly a Black person's term for an aggressive looking lesbian. I had to decide what would be the worst thing to be picked on about between my big lips, tip toe walk or being dubbed a bulldagger. I chose the first two because I was beginning to become immune to teasing about them. Being called gay was a whole new ballgame for me, and I was not ready for that at fourteen, even if it happened to be the truth!

What would be my weapon against being called gay? I had to do something soon because I had already made "Devonne" my new, unofficial best friend. She was the beautiful girl that sat across from me in English class.

That is not her real name by the way. I think its best that I change everyone's name from now. In addition, I want to protect the fact that most of these people had no idea that I was gay in high school. If they did know then, they did not tell me, and they are calling each other now and saying, "I told you she was!" Yeah, right. You only thought you knew! Anyway...

I had thought of a perfect plan to hide my sexuality all throughout high school—*and* remain friends with Devonne, and the rest of the smart, pretty, popular girls. I would pass a love note to as many boys in the school as possible! Not just any boys! I would target the most attractive and popular ones in the school!

I tried to get with the boys that I knew were out of my league—mostly upperclassmen and athletes! That way, I would never have to really go with them or give up any goodies!

Savor this moment! That is the only time in this book that I will use the term "goodies" as it refers to my own.

This is the perfect time to squash another lesbian myth. Not all lesbians hate men! I do not hate men at all. I find it so amusing when they hit on me. I am like, "Dude, do you have a fetish, or a secret fantasy, or something?" I know they can tell I am a lesbian, and that beautiful woman walking beside me is probably my girlfriend, but I don't get stupid about it. I am always cordial to a man that comes up to me or even my girlfriend and makes a pass, as long as they do it in a courteous, respectful manner. During my high school years there were some very handsome, upperclassmen boys. I will give a man his props if he looks good. I just do not want to sleep with or have a relationship with him.

It was so easy! I just kept passing love notes to the popular promiscuous, redbone guy, the linemen on the football team that lived around the corner from me, and the guy that had the coolest car in the parking lot. All of them had girlfriends, but that did not matter to me, as I knew they wouldn't be interested and neither was I! Besides, no one dare called me a bulldagger as I was bold enough to go up to the hottest guys in the school and past them notes right in front of their girlfriends!

The girlfriends did not even bother to fight me because it would be a waste of time for them. They mostly just giggled when I came by and pointed. If the guys were around they would even kiss them in front of me and I would put my head down and rustle up some phony tears. One time I was fake crying over the popular redbone dude and Devonne even gave me a hug for comfort. I hammed it up just so she could hold me longer!

The pass the notes trick worked like a charm and I got through the eighth grade, but something happened that next year. I started getting notes from boys asking me to come under the bleachers! Apparently, the guy with the coolest car in the parking lot lied and told his friends that he had me in the back of his car! He wasn't satisfied with just a younger student passing him notes in front of his girlfriend! He had to go all out and try to make himself look even bigger! My plan had backfired as the *unpopular* upperclassmen boys became increasingly intrigued to get with me because they thought I was easy. *Well, the lesbian secret wasn't out, that's for sure!*

During the hunt for getting Lisa under the bleachers, I met someone during the ninth grade that would become very important in my high school years and beyond. On the way home from school, I found a silver men's ring lying in the parking lot by the Fair Street Grocery. It looked like it could have been real for a second, so I turned to this very tall guy walking nearby and asked him if he thought it was. He quickly said that it looked like a fake, but something made me keep it for many years.

C. Anthony was the first boy that I would ever meet that really carried himself as if he had some sense. He quickly gained the love and trust of my mother, who thought he was just the cat's meow! For me, he was that male friend that I needed to keep me from the vultures! C. Anthony waited for me at the edge of Washington's parking lot to walk me home after school every day, and news quickly spread that we were a couple.

He was in the eleventh grade when I met him, and I learned that the upperclassmen used to dub him as being gay just because he didn't had a girlfriend. A girl cornered me at my locker and said, "Why are you walking home with my boyfriend every day?" She was joking and I was about to hit a girl for the first time ever before she walked off.

C. Anthony was not gay. He just didn't go for little girl's nonsense, and trusted me to be his friend. We dated over the summer and I finally kissed him after we saw Eddie Murphy's *Raw* at the old Rialto movie theatre. It was great being with him just because he was a nice person. I wondered if I would be able to be happy with a boy, even though I had this attraction and desire for girls.

He didn't ask me to go to his junior or senior prom with him, and that was a good thing! Deep down I knew that he wanted a very feminine girlfriend, and that I was just his tomboy best friend.

We both loved basketball with a passion and would stay on the phone for hours talking about it, even though he lived around the corner from me. He would sometime come down to the basketball court at M. Agnes Jones and play with the boys! He's 6'4 and the court was across the street from my house so I couldn't miss him when he was on it. One day I invited him into my room and the unavoidable happened. It would be the first time for both of us. *(Yes, I'm sure it was!)* I had plenty of time to think after that. Could dating a boy and having sex for the first time change everything for me?

After C. Anthony graduated, I was on my own again my junior year. My grades were getting horrible and it was hard to stay in the same classes as Devonne. I had to suck in emotion as Devonne constantly told me about her boyfriend that went to another school.

There is nothing worst than listening to a person talk about how their boyfriend or girlfriend is dogging them out, especially when you really want that person for yourself! You know the agony? Now imagine, if you have to, that you and that person are the same sex! I couldn't help Devonne, and I couldn't place my arms around her like she did me. I felt that she would know that I liked her. I was in so much pain from wanting to be with her one day, that I had to put it in writing. I sat behind her in class and just wrote down my feelings for her.

Devonne I love you so much. I wish that I could tell you that I want to be the one that makes you happy. I would never cheat on you regardless of how far apart we are. I saw the way you looked at one of our friend couples in the hallway. You said that you wished someone could love you like that. I just looked at you, but I wanted to say that I could love you that. I wanted to say it so much, but I can't say anything. I will never say anything, because I know if I do, you would no longer be my friend...

I stopped writing and folded the paper just as we were leaving the classroom. Devonne startled me by doing something I didn't expect her to do. She grabbed the note and asked to read it! I didn't let go of it and told her that she couldn't read it and that it was something very private! It took a few minutes but she finally let the paper go and stopped asking me to read it. She didn't speak to me in our next class.

You talk about breaking a huge sweat! If she had read that I would have been in deep shit! I would accept her pouting attitude over knowing about what I wrote any day! I never wrote anything else about my feelings for her while I was at school. It wouldn't matter. By senior year, my grades were so bad, I was removed from honors classes, and separated from Devonne and the others. I was in the intermediate classes and only saw her at lunchtime.

I had the *misfortune* of meeting an out and proud lesbian transfer in my final year of high school. I say misfortune because all she seemed to want to do was "out" me, and this other boy in our gym class! Once again, I had to see how to combat the gay rumors.

The last plan wouldn't work. I *was* an upperclassman now, and there weren't any boys in my class that I wanted to even front a hit on. It was not because they weren't cute enough or anything like that! It was just that I had known most of them since the sixth grade, and it wouldn't have been convincing at all. I was stuck with the rumors and did not have a counterattack.

The transfer had her girlfriend come up to the school everyday and meet her after classes. Her girlfriend was a Spelman college student and extremely gorgeous! I would hang around after gym just to see the both of them together. I think they knew I was watching and would put on a show just for me—*the closet case in denial!*

It was more than just the physical interaction between them that had me observing. The girlfriend had a small child and I saw a lot of the parenting that they would do. I would find out later that it was the girlfriend that encouraged her younger partner to come back to high school and get her diploma. She said that in order to be with her and to help her to raise her child, the girl had to get her high school diploma. She didn't graduate with me, but eventually she did! The last I heard they were in Michigan and doing quite well together. Good for them! However, it had become obvious that her gay rumors about me had circulated throughout the senior class that year!

There was a special meeting for all seniors in the technical building and I got a rare chance to see Devonne in a group. After dismissal, I went into a little known about girl's bathroom in the building. I heard Devonne ask one of our classmates if that was a bathroom I went into. I also remember hearing them tell her that it was a bathroom just as the door closed behind me.

While I was at the mirror, Devonne walked in. She laughed and said that she never knew that there was a bathroom here. I laughed back and was about to say something pertaining to the meeting we had just left when Devonne suddenly said, "Lisa, don't think that I'm following you or anything, now."

Without a pause and as smooth as I could I said, "No, Devonne, I didn't think that at all."

She quickly left the restroom and I held my head down over the sink. Almost five years of trying to hide myself from my classmates and everyone else around me, but especially from her, all came crashing down on me in that bathroom. She was looking at me in a way that was uncomfortable for her. Not as a good friend anymore, but as one that she should keep her distance from and should try not to give out the wrong signals to.

(However, I'm still to this day a tad puzzled about that incident. She never did use the bathroom after she came in there. So, why again did she come in there? All she did after she came in there was let me know that she wasn't following me)

It was quite clear that my last school days with Devonne wouldn't be like they were with Tracy, but I did experience déjà vu! Devonne was getting ready for a school function and asked me to go into the bathroom with her while she prepared. She had me hold up her jacket while she changed into her dress. I saw her in her undergarments and quickly turned my head. It was more out of disgust, and I hoped I didn't offend her when I did that! I don't even know why I reacted that way. I had dreamed of seeing her naked for five years! But, when I did see her, after that bathroom incident, it didn't have the effect that I thought it would on me. I guess I just respected the fact that she was heterosexual.

Even now, I don't make passes or gestures to heterosexual women because I know that they aren't interested in me, and I am not interested in them. That is another common misconception about dominant lesbians. Not all of us are interested in heterosexual women, and most of us show them respect.

Devonne was my high school crush. I think deep down she always knew that I like her romantically, and I hope she felt that I really cared for her by not looking at her body after I knew that it would make her uncomfortable.

We graduated in full splendor at the Atlanta Civic Center in 1989. In the tradition of Washington High School, we outlined our graduating year in seating arrangement. The white cap and gowned girls were the background and the blue cap and gowned boys were the numbers. (I was in the "9", next to the last row!) My final numbers would be a 2.3 overall GPA. I wasn't an honor student, or queen or debutante or anything special like that. I was just one in the class!

I knew I could have done better in high school and even have been an honor student if I had applied myself more. I just had too much on my mind. Front page editor of the newspaper staff my senior year would be my highest position. Winning the "I Have a Dream" essay contest in my eleventh grade year and receiving a standing ovation from the entire school would be my highest honor!

33

Perry would be disappointed that I wasn't Miss Washington, and that I didn't date the most popular guy in school, or that I didn't make the panel at graduation. My mother and Tim were just glad that I made it out with my diploma. *So was I.*

Mom, Perry and me after my graduation 1989.

This is my niece and me after my graduation in 1989.

Chapter 4

Way too many "Lisas" and still not enough!

My mother had a plan. I was going to be her little girl for the rest of my life. College was just not necessary for me. I had my high school diploma and that is all that mattered to her. Mom only got as far as the eleventh grade at Chamblee High School, but you wouldn't know it. She had business sense about her and had many home ventures for years. However, she never fully recovered after her mastectomy. She also developed thyroid problems and high blood pressure, and was eventually awarded disability assistance. Over the next ten years, her health and well-being would become the prime focus of my life.

The University of North Carolina at Chapel Hill didn't accept me as I had planned for many years. I had dreams to play basketball for the Lady Tar Heels and meet Michael Jordan! I still have the recruiting letter of interest from Coach Hatchell. However, I didn't quite excel in the few games I played at Washington enough to convince the scout that came to see me that I was worth a look! Out went UNC and in came Georgia State University! I didn't even bother to apply to Georgia Tech with a 2.3 GPA and an 890 SAT score. I wasn't too upset. Being the first to go to college in my family was worth more to me. Mom didn't think so, and she let me know the day of my GSU orientation.

"You can get by with just your diploma. That is all you need. Your brothers have good jobs and they didn't waste any money on college. You could use some of that money to help me pay some of these bills!"

I didn't have any money. I got a Pell Grant to pay my tuition, and a book voucher for my books. The grant covered just enough for a full schedule of classes. I chose Psychology as my major and thought about becoming a personal counselor. I didn't know then that by the time we would get to the new millennium, I would be the one that needed counseling!

My first college class was Psychology 101. I walked into a humongous room that looked like a movie theatre in the General Classroom building. It had to be over a hundred students in that class! All different ages and races! That was a big thing for me considering the fact that I grew up in all Black schools. If there was a White person at any of the schools I attended, then they were very smart and extremely popular. I had been brainwashed by one of my mom's borders that all other races were smarter than Black people were. Yes, this did come from a Black person. I had been told that if you were White then you were definitely smarter than I was, and better than me.

There's an old Black folks theory that "if the White folks ain't got it, then it ain't no good!" You'd be surprised at how many Black people still have that way of thinking! I would learn that I was being bamboozled all those years! I had the highest grade in the first class exam and was befriended by other students, both White and Black, who scored less. By the time the professor gave us our first research paper assignment, I didn't even see my college classmate's races anymore. It felt good to drop that feeling of inferiority.

Out of that, at least one hundred students were eight females named Lisa. (*Guiding Light* must have really been popular in the early seventies!) Our professor noticed that none of us shared a common middle name letter and started calling us by our initials. That would be when people began referring to me as, "L.A." It fit me perfectly and has stuck with me every since!

I had my athletic look and cockiness, and it just seemed to gel. I had started to become a familiar face around the gym and Kell Hall and classmates would always stop and ask me something about a class. There was no teasing or worrying about being called a lesbian. These were adults. There was too much emphasis on making good grades in class and the high school shenanigans had been left behind! I was loving college life so much, but someone very dear to me was missing my company.

I had not only stayed in Georgia for college, but I even stayed on the MARTA bus line! Unfortunately, that wasn't enough for my mother. She was totally opposed to me going to college even if I was still in Atlanta and neither one of us was paying for it. It became harder for me to wake up to go to class. I knew she would fake being sick to make me stay home with her. She was sick most of the time, but was *really* sick when I had to go to class. I dropped my only daily class so I did not have to leave her every day. A few weeks later, I dropped another three-day a week class. I told her that I was going to at least continue my Psychology class that quarter because it was my major and only two days a week.

I took a student job in Pullen Library my first year at Georgia State. I was so proud of that $4.00/hr! It was my second job. I got my first job behind my mother's back my senior year at Washington for the Atlanta Journal-Constitution. I sold newspapers at the Five Points MARTA station. I cut a whole day of school getting my Georgia identification and social security cards so that I could work. I got the money needed for the cards by donating blood plasma at the old Boulevard center. They paid $18 for new donors back then.

I wanted to get a job while in high school and my mother refused. I knew she couldn't get the money to pay my senior fees, so I had to do it! Skipping school and hanging in the plasma donation line with the unemployed, drug users and winos was the only way I could get the money to get the credentials needed for my first job. Thank goodness, I only needed my student identification to work in college!

Being a college student also brought excellent opportunities to build, or ruin, my credit rating! They were practically giving away credit cards outside of the student center snack bar. I was awarded a new VISA card with a $600 credit limit just for being a college freshman! I also got my library paycheck the same day and quickly opened a new account at Trust Company Bank. I came home to tell Mom the good news and was disappointed, but not surprised, that she became very upset with me.

"Oh, you think you are a bigshot now! You can go to college and get a bank account and have money in it, when I need your help around here to pay bills and buy food!"

Mom was really feeling the pinch. She only kept a small numbers book commission and had her disability check to support us. She was not receiving any food stamps because I was now over 18 years old. She had obtained a business license and was selling women's items like purses and earrings but earned little money from it.

I chipped in at least half of my money to her even with my first paycheck, but it was not enough to keep up with mom's desire for a nice looking household. Our house was always nice back in the seventies and eighties, which is why mom did so much entertaining. Once you are used to nice things it's hard to let that lifestyle go. My mom wasn't materialistic, but she did like to keep new furniture and appliances in the house.

Since we didn't have the money to buy the furniture, my mom got tangled into the home rental service's web. She would have weekly and monthly furniture and appliance bills from Easy Rental, Network Rental, Love Rental, Curtis Mathes and you name it! Those would put hundreds of dollars more in our expenses in addition to the rent and utilities. We were always at least one or two hundred dollars behind what we needed and had to hope for a "number" miracle or that mom would get a big sale from her business.

It would take years to finally pay those accounts off, and once we did get at least one paid off, I would come home to a new television set or stereo system in the living room.

"Mom, why did you get something else? We just paid off the bedroom set. This is only bringing in another bill!" It was the same reason every time.

"The salesman cut down our other payments if we agreed to add this on. We are only paying an extra $10 a month to add this to our bill."

(Add the fact that my mom thought that the both the Network and Easy rental sales representatives were extremely good looking, and you can imagine how their deals were hard for her to resist.)

Although the new contracts would cut our payments down a few dollars every month, they would also add an additional 18 months to pay it all off. The rental sales representatives would keep us in the game longer by cutting the monthly cost, and delivering another item. Most of the time my mom wouldn't even see the stuff she was ordering until it arrived at our house! That's how much she trusted these sales representatives! She was a very smart woman and great with her businesses, but somehow she became intrigued with the Rent-To-Own industry as a consumer and just couldn't get enough of it, or the sales representatives! Tim and I would feel the pressure of picking up the payments. Sometimes it would turn into a heated family argument.

One night mom brought up that I could help more around the house if I quit school and got a full time job. Tim responded by reminding her about how she had it made with taking care of me throughout school because of my *athletic* appearance. She could always go to the cheap stores and buy my school clothes because I never demanded the popular name brand attire that other girls wanted. He was saying that she saved hundreds of dollars every year that allowed her to keep rental furniture and appliances in the household. It was one of the few times that Tim would speak up for me to our mother.

That first quarter at Georgia State, I received a "C" average in Psychology 101 after having a perfect grade in the first two weeks. I lost my job at Pullen Library and went default on my Pell Grant both because I had to be a full time student in order to receive work and grant benefits. I became a part time student after I dropped my other two classes. I had chose three classes for the next quarter to keep my eligibility and possibly return to my library job position but things got worst at home.

After being late four months in a row, the property owner decided not to renew our lease and we had to move. The only way to raise enough money to stay at our new apartment was for me to get a full time job and leave college. So I did. There were way too many "Lisas" in Psychology 101, but just not enough at home.

Chapter 5

High School Was Better

I was already a college dropout at the start of the nineties and quickly became a part of the work force. After failed attempts in customer service and hotel room service, I found a place in the security and investigations industry. I would spend years as both an armed and unarmed licensed security professional. My second position in security would be at Lenox Mall. I was given the job even though at the time I didn't know how to drive, which was required for certain posts. I guess the director of security really believed in my ability as a fast learner!

A lot was happening when I got my job at Lenox. President George Bush would deploy troops to Iraq for Operation Desert Shield; I would see a DVD player for the first time for $800, and my mother was about to lose yet another source of income!

After trying for years, Georgia voters would finally agree to a statewide lottery, causing a slow end to the illegal number racket. My mom lost her commission book as soon as Cash 3 machines arrived at the corner store. Why pay the illegal lottery and risk the bookie not paying you if the state guarantees you payment at any lottery retailer if you win? Number players slowly chose to play the state lottery for guaranteed payment even though the illegal number had a higher payout rate.

Mom just had her monthly disability check and any sales that she made from her business. She got lucky and landed a huge Christmas time account from the Extra Point Men's Club to buy all of their toys for their holiday toy drive but that wasn't enough. We still had those rental company furniture and appliance bills to pay. I was glad that my new job paid a good, steady weekly salary.

I can honestly say that I didn't see what happened next coming. I had graduated from high school, went to college, and had thought ridicule and ignorance was behind me. I'm afraid that it wasn't so!

I was wearing my mall security officer's uniform when I caught the number 13 bus to ride downtown. Even though I was in officer's clothing, I still had a woman's appearance. I had my hair in a short, but still a unisex style, and wore small earrings. I waited for the bus near the Clark Atlanta University along with about ten other women and a Black man in a business suit.

When the bus arrived, the man stepped to the side and allowed all the women to enter the bus before him. I was the last one to walk to the bus steps. As I was about to board, the man bombarded his way in front of me! What was he doing? Was he implying that I wasn't woman enough for him to let go in front of him? What the hell kind of chivalry was that?

We became entangled as I didn't stop boarding, and neither did he, and crossed arms as we swiped our MARTA cards through the fare reader. The bus driver was in awe, as most of the passengers! We didn't say a word, or jerk or push each other out of the way. It was one of the smoothest acts of rudeness that you could ever witness without a word being said. We took our seats, the bus driver laughed, shook his head and we rode downtown.

I didn't ask him to let me on the bus before him. I didn't ask him to be a *gentleman* for me at all! But, the fact that he allowed ten other women to enter the bus before I did, and that he decided not to let me on only after he saw that I was not wearing a dress and heels like they were, was appalling! Chivalry is not dead only if I look like *you* want me to look. That's BS!

Out of the eight officers that worked the mall security day shift, I was one of only two women. The other female, Paula, had seniority over me and was a favorite of the male officers, especially this one named Charles. It was like being in the military or on a football team. We had a locker room where we changed together and everything. The guys were used to Paula changing in front of them and would make the usual whistling sounds. She would enjoy the attention. I, of course, didn't enjoy getting undressed in front of the men and would retreat into a storage room to change.

Just because I wasn't as open to them as Paula was, the male officers starting beaming me around as a dyke to the staff at the mall. Suddenly, high school didn't seem all that bad! I tried a similar plan to the one I had in high school and went out on a date with one of the men on the cleaning staff. Since the cleaning guy only got as far as first base on our evening out, he added to the dyke rumors more than helping them!

He even started another rumor that I was secretly into Paula. I tried to talk to her and let her know that it was nonsense, but she wouldn't even allow me to come near her and threatened to inform our supervisor if I did. She even requested to be posted away from any area I worked each day to the watch scheduler. I didn't know what to do.

I was having lunch in the food court and one of the senior housekeeping males came up to me that knew about the teasing.

"Why does it bother you so much that they are calling you a lesbian? I know and you know that it is true, right?"

I wanted to smack him in the jaw, but he approached me in a very respectful manner and I stayed polite.

"I've never been with a woman before and even if I did it wouldn't be a woman like Paula! I've even been out with a person that worked here and they are still saying this about me. The only reason why I haven't quit is because I really need this job."

He quickly sat down and encouraged me not to quit my position. He also told me that he could relate to what I was going through because his daughter is a lesbian and had problems dealing with her sexuality. He even showed me a picture and asked if I wanted to meet her! I looked at him funny. He just laughed and stood up.

"It took her five years to finally come out to me. Just let me know if you change your mind. I think you would be good for her and she would be for you."

She was very attractive and I was interested, but I didn't let him know that. The way he knew so much I don't even think I had to!

After about two months, the gay bashing was getting excessively much for me to handle alone. I needed another C. Anthony to rescue me! I just happened to find him in a fifty-two year old man named William. He worked as a restaurant cleaner for Micks. I wasn't attracted to William at all. I just needed someone to curb the rumors and give me a sense of security. He made a lot of money and even offered to help me get back into school at Georgia State. I had told him about the deficiency in my student account and he offered to pay it immediately. I was only twenty-one at the time and very naïve, so I started dating this man thirty years my senior.

Besides the huge age difference there was another downside to my relationship with William. He was an old school heroin junkie turned crack cocaine addict living in the rough Sylvan area of Atlanta! I would go to his house after work and would have to keep tons of crack fiend women from coming into his apartment. My reward was well more than my weekly Lenox salary, but the price to pay for being his girlfriend was horrendous. I had only been intimate with two other men since C. Anthony, and one was from an assault a year earlier. It was tougher for me to be with William than with the unknown man that raped me. *(I know that's quite harsh to say, but its true)*

Dealing with the crack women and the bad sex was only the tip of the iceberg with William. He had an ongoing feud with a neighbor, whom after he had slept with his wife, fired rounds into his apartment only moments after I had left one evening. I had to answer phone calls on the hour from his wife in Florida about missed child support payments for his son while I was there. He would have frightening Vietnam flashbacks where he would lose all site of where he was and begin looking for the enemy! I had to constantly remind him that I was on *his* side! Finally, he would insist that after all the post Vietnam testicular surgery, (long story about what happened there), and that he had not conceived a child in over twenty years, I didn't have to worry about using birth control.

Dating William may have helped my financial situation, but it did nothing for the problems I had working security at the mall. Charles was beginning to hate me more and more for no apparent reason. Paula consistently refused his advances, and somehow he seemed to blame me for his inability to woo her! Charles was about 6'3, 340 pounds, married and with children, which made me really have no idea why he was pursuing this woman so much!

One day, dispatch called me to deliver a wheelchair to the information booth. I was far away on the North end of the mall so I asked the operator to call the closest officer to pick up the chair. That just happened to be Charles that day. He was furious that dispatch requested him to assist and called me to the back office some time later. When I entered the office, he immediately grabbed me and jacked me up against the wall!

"You want to be a man? Be a man, then! Don't you ever have someone tell me to do your job again! I ain't your boy!"

I had stopped growing in the ninth grade. I am about 5'9, and at that time, I only weighed about 140 pounds so you can imagine how I was floating in the air with his hands around my neck. Lenox wrote the incident up and we were issued warnings, but not suspensions and neither one of us were fired. I didn't file any formal charges, although co-workers wished I had.

We were separated from each other as frequently as possible by the watch scheduler. A few weeks later Charles took a stab at both women on the shift during a staff meeting.

"If you would hire fewer women and fake men then we could get more work finished and not have to worry about baby sitting."

Although he was clearly a womanizer and a horrible person, he was valuable to asset to mall security because he was large guy that could cause a would-be shoplifter to think twice! Paula and I couldn't compete with that, so we remained quiet to keep our jobs.

William didn't react to the incident with Charles. By that time, I was avoiding intercourse with him more and more and he eventually got tired of me. He had promised to give me some money for a class I was taking so I came to his house that evening.

When I got there, he had a bunch of women in his living room passing crack pipes. He immediately told me to leave and that they were smoking the money that he was going to give me. I told him that the money wasn't the only reason that I was coming to see him.

I was two months pregnant. He quickly dismissed all indication that the baby was his, and tossed me down his apartment steps.

"Well, that's life," He said. "You are gay too, and you just don't know it yet! I have plenty of women in here that can satisfy me."

I caught the bus home and cried all the way. I had played with fire and just been burned. I should have never talked to this man at all and I certainly shouldn't have been running his house and spending his money even if he was allowing me to do so. I went back to his house two days later and everything was gone from the apartment. He had moved away.

About two months later, due to the pregnancy and the animosity I resigned from my security position. I didn't inform anyone at corporate about the pregnancy so everyone just thought it was because of the incident with Charles. He would brag that he was the cause of me leaving the job for weeks. It took a long time before they hired another female to work the same shift with him. Just before I went into the hospital to have the baby, I ran into one of my former mall security co-workers. The secret was out, as then I weighed well over 200 pounds!

"So, that's the real reason you left Lenox isn't it? I'm glad. All of us thought that it was just because of Charles."

I really did like the job and would have probably stayed until I got maternity leave if not for Charles being on the same shift.

"I wished that I could have worked there a little longer. I could have used the money. They made me angry because they never fired him for doing what he did to me. He was still able to work and downsize women everyday if he'd want to. That wasn't fair at all and he's still getting a big paycheck every week while being an asshole!"

My former co-worker pointed to the black strip of tape around his badge that I hadn't noticed. "He's not getting paid anything now."

Charles had died from a heart attack. When I got home later that day, I had two messages on my answering machine from my former boss. My co-worker had obviously called him and let him know about the pregnancy. Paula had also left, and I was being offered my old job after my recovery.

Chapter 6

Reasons to Live

My aunt Rene was the first to tell me that she saw two heartbeats in my neck. That is an old wife's tale way to see if a woman is pregnant. Mom and her friends always believed in those. I remember when one of them was sick and needed an ice pick and a bucket of water to put under her bed to help the illness. I have no idea to this day what the heck that was for! Before I was even six months pregnant, I was told that the baby would be a girl and that she would have all the traits of my late grandmother, Lizzie. They wouldn't be too far from the truth!

William was gone without a trace and I had to go through my pregnancy without the father. Mom was there more than I could ever imagine and I finally had learned her secret wish. She always wanted this to happen to me. She wanted me to have a baby that she could raise and for me to get welfare assistance to help. A baby meant WIC milk, food stamps, a monthly check and Medicaid health benefits.

She had raised my brothers and me on assistance for years and thought that it would be my silver lining. I told her that I wanted to go to college and not take handouts from the government. I also told her that we were moving into a state of welfare reform and that the opportunities that she had raising us were soon to become obsolete. Of course, she didn't believe me.

Vee, my first daughter, was born exactly on her due date in March of 1992. She weighed a very healthy seven pounds and one ounce! Times had changed at Grady Hospital and I was released with her after just 48 hours of observation. Mom had the room decked out for me as if I was still in the hospital. She had fresh new sheets and the bed ready when I came home. It was clear that she didn't want me to lift a finger. I slept most of the day and she held Vee like a sack full of money all day long! You couldn't pry my baby out of her hands! I almost had to beg her to let me hold my own child!

My daughter was a celebrity in our apartments the first weeks after her birth. I didn't even know most of the neighbors that brought her diapers and onesies as gifts. Only the big pink ribbon on the door let them know that there was a new baby in the house!

I was happy being a mother and was determined to give my daughter opportunities that I wouldn't able to take advantage of. I remember telling her while rocking her to sleep, (a rare moment that I would enjoy only after my brothers convinced my mother to let me do it for once), that she would go to college and that I would never hold her back from her dreams.

I turned down the security job offer at Lenox Mall after Vee was born. More than anything, I wanted to get back into school. I felt that if I had returned to the workforce then I would be trapped in the dead end job, single parent, living paycheck-to-paycheck routine! I decided to go back to Georgia State that summer and earn my degree while receiving government assistance for my mother to take care of my daughter. My Pell grant was reinstated and I was back in class with a full schedule again. I received a very small monthly welfare allowance. So small that I don't even remember the amount! It really didn't matter because all of it and my food stamps went to my mother for keeping Vee while at was at school.

Things were going well for a while. My mother was satisfied with Vee at home keeping her company and I attended school at GSU that first summer session. I was even trying to date C. Anthony from time to time for a little recreation. He didn't mind that I had a daughter now. We were never as serious as people wanted us to or made us out to be. I was just a good friend for hanging out. He even gave me my first driving lesson after I made a 3.2 average in my classes at GSU. I was making better grades than high school and there was not much pressure.

Just before I registered for second summer session, we had a change in household situation. One of Tim's ex-girlfriends was killed in the now defunct East Lake Meadows housing project by her drug dealer boyfriend. She had four surviving young children, including my then ten year old nephew, Junior. All of the children were separated into different homes. My brother was not able to have Junior move into his home at the time, so he came to live with us. My mother and I saw it as an opportunity for us to get closer to Junior, and help him spend his school years in a more positive environment.

Of course, a child doesn't grow up in a house where his mother and her boyfriend were drug dealers without coming out tarnished! His mother's customers also inhabited the house where he lived. We would hear chilling stories of unsuitable events that my nephew witnessed. A social worker would also tell us about a gay male friend of Junior's mother who would care for the children while she went out to sell drugs. For the first time in my life, I would hear my mother use an inappropriate homosexual term to one of her friends over the phone referring to this person. It became clear that my mother did not like gay people, and I had to shove my true self even more into the closet!

Junior had problems with his temper and was constantly suspended from school after he came to live with us. My mother was beginning to have more on her plate to handle with him and Vee to care for. She had no problems with my returning to school the first summer session, but after my nephew's arrival, we would have old familiar arguments.

We also had to move into a three-bedroom apartment, as Junior needed his own room. The move would add an additional $700 per month to our expenses, including the fact that we had to get another bedroom set. Of course, mom rented that! I had no choice but to leave school again. I dropped my classes, forfeited my Pell grant and welfare assistance and returned to work in the security field.

Don't get me wrong. I wasn't upset about this at all! My nephew and his siblings were in the house when their mother was fatality shot in the head by this man. They needed us, especially Junior, since he was the oldest, and with his mother longer.

It took only one paycheck after I started working again and we moved into a three-bedroom apartment in Collier Heights. It was a nice apartment and we all had our own rooms and space. We just could never enjoy it! There was never any peace as feuds that started miles away ended at our apartment. My brother's girlfriends would track them to our home and cause ruckus in the parking lot. My mother's boyfriend would make her blood pressure rise with his infidelities and my Aunt Rene would keep my mother up until dawn wanting to play cards. Vee would cry and have me walking the hallway after I returned from work until the wee hours. I needed a rest very soon.

I finally got my first break from the job during my twenty-second birthday. I had three days off. C. Anthony had started seriously dating a woman he worked with at the Airport and couldn't take me out. I was really upset and stopped speaking to him for a long time. I spent my birthday playing cards with mom and Aunt Rene. Fate played a hand that night that would change my life yet again.

There was a knock on the door at around 9:00 PM that evening. It was the apartment courtesy officer.

"Is someone here driving a burgundy Grand Marquis? Someone just tried to steal your car!"

The car belonged to my Aunt Rene. We both came to the door and you could see her car, still running, almost out of the apartment complex driveway! They had wired the vehicle and the courtesy officer had caught them. They got away on foot and left the car because they couldn't control it!

Aunt Rene was notorious for driving her hoopties, and this one had a problem with the steering wheel locking up where only she knew how to use a screwdriver to fix it. It was better than buying a steering wheel club, because it worked even after the car was in motion!

They damaged the interior of the vehicle and we needed a police report. I stood outside talking to Bernard, the courtesy officer, for hours waiting on the police to come. I told him it was my birthday and how disappointed that I was that I didn't go out to celebrate. He said that he was newly single and had one son that he wasn't allowed to see. We both had sob stories and decided that we would get to know each other. He instantly offered to take me out for my birthday the next day. We saw each other every day I had off from work that week.

After 6 years, C. Anthony had begun to change. He had a new girlfriend now, and had shed the image of being the quiet nerd he was in high school. After he had his first real girlfriend, he didn't need his little gal pal hanging around him anymore.

Bernard was very nice and I quickly replaced C. Anthony with him as my new good friend. He also enjoyed being around Vee, and we would be seen at Underground Atlanta pushing her in her stroller up and down Peachtree Street almost every evening.

There used to be a restaurant called Texas near GSU in the early nineties. During the day, it was just a restaurant, but at night, it became a lesbian nightspot. Some of the women would hang around Underground Atlanta after leaving Texas and people watch. Bernard and I strolled by one night with Vee and I caught the eye of one of the women. She was beautiful! I stared at her for a while and looked away only after Bernard kept me from walking into a pole! I knew that I was still living a life that was a lie and no man could change that, no matter how nice he was.

In the first week of October, I started to cry all the time. I cried at work and at home and even cried myself to sleep at night. I went to a doctor on my work plan and he said that I was going through a first trimester depression. Vee was only five months old, and I was pregnant with another child by Bernard. My mother got a chance to do another happy dance. It seemed that it didn't matter how many children I gave birth to, just as long as she was able to take care of them!

Perry was not so elated. He was dismayed by me having another child so soon after Vee. I wasn't too disappointed. I had wanted to have a boy so that Vee would have a little brother. In fact, this pregnancy was planned. Bernard was upset that he couldn't see his son and wanted me to have a child for him. I agreed, obviously not knowing what I would be getting myself into.

The owner of the security company I was working for found out that I was pregnant, and I was laid off. He said that he didn't want a pregnant woman working security no matter how early it was. I worked for him in a very bad area, so I respected him for that. I couldn't get unemployment because I hadn't worked long enough, so I asked Bernard if he would help pick up the slack since I was pregnant with his child. He would do so, but at a huge price. He moved into my bedroom in my mother's house with me so that he didn't have to pay rent at the rooming house were he lived.

That is when our problems began. It would be only a few months before he started to want to run the streets with his friends, and not have enough money for the house. I would hear it from my mother and brothers for months that he would turn out to be a freeloader that knocked me up.

Just before my second trimester, I told Bernard that we needed to get an apartment of our own. Since he had moved in, my mother had made comments that she only had the responsibility of taking care of Junior and herself. She considered us as another family, and deep down I knew she was right. Bernard agreed that we could move in together, but that he thought that I should get an abortion. I was pissed off tremendously! First, you ask me to get pregnant for you and then when you see how much of a responsibility it is to raise a family, you ask me to terminate the pregnancy this late?

I won't lie to you and say that I didn't arrange to do so. I am pro-choice. I don't think that you should bring a child into this world unless you plan to take care of them. I even booked an appointment at the old Midtown Clinic. I remember riding the bus to get an abortion that day, and passing on by the clinic crying. I rode the bus back to the station and went home. I confronted Bernard the next evening and told him that I couldn't do it. I can still see the look on his face.

"You asked me to have your child and I am going to do it. You will just have to accept the responsibility. William pushed me down his steps and denied my first baby, and you knew that when you asked me to have yours. I am not going to let this child down and neither are you."

In July of 1993, after two weeks of slow, hard labor, my daughter Tee was born. She was as beautiful as her sister was and weighed seven ounces more at birth! Bernard didn't get another son, but he was extremely glad that he had a little girl and thanked me for staying on that bus. I would now always have reasons for living.

Chapter 7

Unhappily Married, (Part 1)

Whenever I talk to people about my first apartment, I'm usually referring to when I moved downtown to 710 Peachtree. That was actually the first time I lived *alone*. My actual first apartment away from my mother was when Bernard, the girls and I moved into a two bedroom in Collier Heights just across the courtyard from her. This would be my attempt at living a heterosexual common law married life. I trusted Bernard even more than I trusted C. Anthony, and he was the father of one of my children. He also didn't have a problem getting up and going to work, and that was very important!

Bernard still worked as an armed security officer and I had to make sure that he kept his weapons in a place where the girls couldn't find them. I had to Mary Poppins the whole place actually! I tried to cook meals and keep the house clean for us. It didn't work out well at all! I was not the domestic housewife, and I hated the thought of becoming one. It wasn't because of the duties, but because of the fact of whom I was partnered with. Bernard is good person, but he is a man. That is not who I wanted to take care of. These would be hard times for me, and I would cry on a daily basis. Things would only get worse.

My common law husband wasn't romantic at all after we moved in together! I gave him a box of candy, a white rose and a gold wristwatch for Valentines Day, and he decided that he'd rather hang out with the boys. I was so pissed off that I walked out of the house and was on the way to my mothers. Well, actually I didn't make it to her apartment. I stopped midway. I had showed her my gifts for him earlier and she had already told me that they wouldn't effect Bernard one bit! I didn't want to hear an "I told you so", and she was more than ready to give me one! I turned around and came back to our apartment.

Bernard had already left to go meet whom he was hanging out with. I was locked out of the house. Was it by accident? I never asked him. I climbed into the bedroom window and saw that the candy I gave him was on the edge of the dresser, the rose was on the floor in front, and the gold watch was behind the dresser! That was clearly a sign that he had thrown the items into the room before he left. He gave me nothing that holiday. I spent the whole night thinking about how I would've made *my wife* very happy every Valentine's day!

I had both of my daughters in my lap as we watched Charlotte Smith hit that shot at the buzzer to give the North Carolina women their NCAA basketball championship in 1994. I saw that coming years ago! Coach Hatchell had done what I knew she would! I would've been a senior on that team with Smith, Marion Jones, Sylvia Crawley and Tonya Sampson if I could've gotten into Carolina. Maybe I would played and hit that shot! It wouldn't have been as spectacular though. I was living Charlotte's dream and she accomplished it perfectly! It was for a different school from her uncle David Thompson, but the same results and even the same championship score, 60-59! It was sports book picture perfect! I looked around my house after the game. It wasn't even Polaroid picture worthy.

I was so depressed about being around the house everyday, I decided to go back to work. Bernard wanted to take care of all the bills and the rent and I was just supposed to stay home and take care of cooking, cleaning and the babies. After he saw how much money it would take for diapers, milk, clothes and toys, we finally agreed for me to get a job. I went to work in security for the Atlanta Housing Authority. I kept the girls clothed and fed, and was even able to pay my mom some money for babysitting. She really needed the money too, since she remained in that three-bedroom apartment after we moved out.

The next month we had some serious bill and domestic trouble. I received past due notices from the utility companies and our apartments. I found out that Bernard had a money management problem. He denied that he didn't pay the bills and said that the utility companies were the ones with the record problems. I asked to see the receipts and we had a big argument! He said that he would take care of it, and not to worry about it.

We also argued about my housework, or lack thereof, after I returned to work. So, now we were both working and I had to come home and still take care of the children, and cook and clean all alone? I checked my undershirt for an "S"! He clearly expected me to be Superwoman!

Some days after our housework argument, I got a phone call from a woman that was selling Avon that I had met on my job. She had also met Bernard, and knew that we were in a relationship. While I was trying to order some items for my mother, she said that Bernard had made a pass at her. Her exact words were that he said that he was about to "fire the woman of the house". *Oh, really?*

I told him of the incident and we didn't argue about it. He just denied it and we moved on. I still bought my mom's Avon from her too. (Word to the wise: When your mate doesn't make a big deal out of something like that, be very concerned! Come to think of it, what man hangs out with his boys on Valentine's Day, anyway? I think I had been sacked since that night anyway!)

The camel's back broke a few months later. It was June 17, 1994. I couldn't forget this date for several reasons. I was talking to my mother on the phone and we were suddenly disconnected. When, then Southern Bell, used to shut off your phone service, you could only call 911 in case of trouble, or their office to make a payment to turn it back on! Sure enough, our phone was disconnected with a bill deficit. I went across the courtyard to my mother's house to let her know about the phone. On my way back to my apartment, I noticed a pink slip of paper tacked to our door. Our rent was past due and we had a warrant to move! I ran into the house to call Bernard and got even more pissed! *I had forgotten that the phone was off!*

I turned on the television set to get my mind off the fact that I was so upset with my common law husband, and saw the marquee event of that day!

O.J. Simpson was being slowly chased by the police in that white Bronco! I watched the chase for about ten minutes with the rest of the nation, when the television set and my air conditioner both went off! I quickly went outside and was met with the Georgia Power technician who said that the electric bill hadn't been paid in two months! I told him that I had been watching the police chase and he ran back to his truck and drove off. *Obviously to find an establishment that had power to view the end of it!*

Bernard came home later to find me sitting in the dark. I had left the girls over to my mothers. The first thing he wanted to talk about the police chase, but I wasn't in the mood at all. I had a warrant to move, and two utilities that I thought had been paid, shut off on me in the same day!

A historic day for the nation that will be remembered as the day of the O.J. Simpson police chase will be forever marked as the last straw for me in being a domesticated, heterosexual housewife to a non-romantic man!

I'm sure after reading what happened above that some would quickly say that my bad experience with Bernard, William and other men would be the reason I *turned* or *chose* to be a homosexual. You'd be only partially right. I chose to stop denying my homosexuality after these events.

I've always had an attraction for women and a desire to be in domestic relationship with a woman. Even if Bernard had paid those bills and had brought me something that Valentine's Day, then it would still have just been a matter of time before I left him. I wasn't happy with a man and I was never going to be. I just knew then that I was so tired of being someone else.

I had absolutely no idea what I was about to experience in discovering the homosexual community and myself. I had the attitude of "Was the gay world ready for me?"

The real question should have been "Was I ready?"

Chapter 8

Was The Gay World Ready? *(Was I?)*

There should have been some sort of book for me to refer to when coming out. *JohnTre's Guide to Sexual Orientation & Acceptance in the U.S.* would have been perfect for me to read back then. I would have known what I was supposed to have been looking for when I placed my first woman seeking woman personal ad in the newspaper. As I recalled, it read:

"Black female seeks an attractive, multi-cultured female of any race for a first time encounter and possible relationship. Must like children and animals."

That was just not the right advertisement for me! I tried to put out that multi-cultured females are what I'm attracted to without coming off as shallow. I just like women with a lot of variety about themselves. I like variety in any race, but knew I could probably find it more in a woman that had been exposed to many different environments. I knew more of what I was attracted to back then, and just went with that. I got about ten responses that evening alone. Most of them were Black women cursing me out!

"You are just like those brothers that only like those light skinned, long haired women! Why didn't you just say that you want a white woman in your ad?"

That was just not the response that I was hoping for.

A woman answered that said she had an Italian uncle, and had lived briefly in Italy. She didn't like the fact that I was "bicurious", and made that known. She really didn't like to teach anyone the ropes. I was always cocky about my sexual performance even when with men, so I told her that she wouldn't have to teach me anything in bed—but I did have to ask her what the heck did "bicurious" mean!

"It means that you have never been with a woman before. You still live with a man, and you are looking to meet a woman. That's being bicurious."

I countered that I wasn't having sex with Bernard, and it was just a temporary living arrangement that we were together. She said that I was still "bicurious". I then asked her what I would be if I had sex with her, and she said "bisexual", just like her!

Oh, ok. Knowledge is power! So, I was talking to a bisexual woman. That was **NOT** a good thing for me, and I would find that out when I met her for lunch!

"Oh my God, I have got to get out of here!" she said when I walked into the restaurant and sat down at her table. *Gee, was it the big lips thing again, I wondered?*

"What's wrong? I'm not your type?" She was mine, though. A very beautiful woman that spoke a little Italian, and I had enjoyed our telephone conversations.

"No. You are not bicurious, bisexual or "bi" anything! You are a flat out lesbian! I can't be seen with you or my congregation will know something. Don't call me anymore, please. Sorry, take care."

She then got up and left me in the restaurant to each lunch alone. (Oh, yes, she was a minister in case you noticed she said *congregation*).

I was called a flat out lesbian! Not a bulldagger or a dyke, but a lesbian! What the heck *was* a lesbian, and why was I not passable as bi? Did I *want* to be passable as bi? Why would that be such a problem? There were closets and causes about being a homosexual that I clearly did not know about.

I began talking to another woman that answered my ad. Sabrina was an older woman and did not care that I "looked like a lesbian", as the pastor had put it. Sabrina said that she was whom I needed. She said I didn't need to start a relationship right off the bat and that I would be headed for disaster if I did. I met her that night after work and she came home with me. My first sexual encounter with a woman was wonderful and felt very natural. I wasn't at all surprised. I was disappointed that it wasn't love, though. It was just to satisfy curiosity, and end all doubts. That is what it did. Sabrina was my first, and a one-night stand, as she quickly got back home to fix dinner!

Bernard came home that evening and for some odd reason wanted to touch me. I rejected his advance and I told him that I would move back in with my mother at the end of the month. We were still in the eviction process. I also told him that I would take care of the girls and that he could get a room in a boarding house and have little responsibility, which is what he wanted. We made a child support agreement that we still have to this day for our daughter.

I had always promised Bernard two things. One is that he would be the last man to ever touch me, and second that I would never take our child support matter into the courts if he did the right thing by our daughter. I didn't completely come out to him that evening, but I'm sure he wondered why I gave him that first promise!

Sabrina told me that I could save my money from placing personal ads in the newspaper and turned me on to this woman-to-woman chat line. I quickly met Lynda, who was Puerto Rican and only a few years older than I was. Lynda would be a short, but very important encounter for me in learning more about where I would fit into homosexuality. I met her at Underground Atlanta for our first date.

I was extremely nervous about meeting her, especially after my "flat out lesbian" episode with the bisexual, closeted clergywoman. It was little better with Lynda. I wasn't very attracted to her, but I liked the fact she had lived in San Juan, and spoke some Spanish. She had a great family and was out to them. That would have been perfect except there was something that else I didn't know about myself!

Lynda was very cocky—almost as cocky as I was—and she wasn't very romantic. I bought her some roses and she rejected them. I had always wanted to buy a woman some roses just for anything! I bought some for her and got the same reaction as when I bought them for Bernard! What gives?

She came to my house while I was packing up and started to take out my garbage. I told her that wasn't necessary, and she said that if we were going to be together than I wouldn't have to do stuff like that anymore. I liked that for a minute and was buying it until she said,

"I just want you to take care of the kids and be a good *housewife*. Just like you were to Bernard, and he didn't care. He didn't know how to treat you as a wife but I do!"

Whoa! Something got twisted! I wasn't looking for a *replacement* for Bernard! I was looking to take Bernard's *place* in a relationship! Was I was doing something wrong?

Sabrina was there to clear it up for me, because as I mentioned earlier, I didn't have a book to refer to! She laughed her butt off and tried to explain to me what had happened.

"I knew it wouldn't work! You are both the same type of lesbian! You are both butches with butch role playing tendencies! That never works as a couple!"

There are *types* of lesbians? I had no idea! I just thought if a woman wanted a woman, then she would date a woman. No. There is role play, there are duties, and there are norms that are expected by some. I was a "butch", or "stud", or a term for a dominant lesbian. Yes sir, I was the heterosexual stereotype of all lesbians! I was one of those that look like men, and sometimes take male-like duties of the relationship, which was why I couldn't be seen with the preacher woman. Everyone would know! That is also why I was always so obviously lesbian, even in high school to the outside world! I actually look gay! It was all starting to make sense to me—well, sort of anyway.

Sabrina and her friends liked to go to the Marquette Club on M.L. King Drive. The "Sleazy Queasy" was the Black gay shrine of the hood! I heard my mom talk about Mr. Hunter, the owner all the time! He was good friends back in the day with both my mother and father when she would be a regular at the Busy Bee. The club used to sit in the old historic Black Peachtree Street area of M.L. King, across from the original Paschals, the Busy Bee and The Carousel restaurants, and down the street from the famous Alecks Barbecue Heaven.

That area is only a memory to old school Atlantans, with a huge Publix grocery store slapped where the old club and Alecks used to be. The Marquette Club moved to Simpson Road, and Mr. Hunter has since passed away, but all of us oldies remember the first building, and I will never forget my first night inside when I officially came out!

I went downtown after work to pick up some coming *out* clothes. I selected a black pair of men's slacks and a shirt from New York Men's Fashions near Five Points. I wasn't shy at all about going in there and picking out something to wear. It was the first time that I walked into a men's store and shopped for myself! It felt great and the clerks were very nice to me. I called Sabrina when I got home and told her that I was ready to go. She had lined up two women that wanted to go out with me! I talked with them both, and they were ok about me having two dates for the evening. *How cool was that?*

I walked up those tall red-carpeted stairs into the Marquette Club with two women under my arm. Both of my dates were nice looking. They wore dresses and heels and had on makeup. I was elated! I would find out later that they would be classified as, "femmes". My dates weren't frisked going through the door—but I was! That was interesting. What were they implying?

I looked around and saw women with women and men with men! I got a little pep in my step! I was a little kid in a completely new magical place of expression. I had almost forgotten about my dates! I quickly got them to a booth near the stage.

Ok, what was I supposed to do next? Oh, yes! Offer to buy them a drink! That's it! They both wanted a glass of white wine.

I went to the bar and was met by a woman that was dressed in men's clothing such as I was.

(Sorry, for playing with words here, but just in case you do not have a copy of *JohnTre's Guide to Sexual Orientation & Acceptance in the U.S.*, and do not understand just quite yet, I am walking you through some homosexual terminology and role play)

This was another "butch" lesbian, or "stud" and we greeted each other with a little dap, or a hand gesture. I had a "femme" come up to me at the bar and asked me where I got my clothes. I told her, and she quickly scooted in front of me, which I thought was quite rude, until Sabrina came up. She gave me a hug and the "femme" walked away without a drink.

"So, two dates not enough for you?" I looked at her confused and she continued, "There's just no hope for you, is it? That woman was flirting with you! That's why she got in front of you like that!"

I didn't have a clue. Butches aren't men, but in the homosexual world, butches are the closest counterparts to heterosexual men. We are for the most part, as blind as bats to see the females that are interested, and quick to run to the ones that pick us bone dry! The butch ego is closely related to the male ego, and it is easy to strike the wrong nerve to some. I would find those traits to be reasons some femme lesbians will shy away from us as well!

Sabrina went back to her table and I brought the drinks back to the booth. I felt like the guy in those beer commercials sandwiched between two women. They were very nice girls, but someone else caught my interest. I saw a woman at the club that night that I would never see again. She was so beautiful and sitting with another butch. That butch was dogging her out! I could tell from across the club that they were having an argument. I think that's when the hero side of me started to surface! I wanted to rescue a woman and become her Prince Charming! Boy, I'd be asking for it for the next decade or so!

Ask most people who was the first drag queen that they ever saw and they probably will say Rupaul or Lady Chablis. For me, it would be that night in the Marquette Club when I saw Sheresa Labelle! I had my mouth open when she came out! A man that totally looked like a woman in every way. I fell in love with drag shows after that! She announced to the crowd that she saw so many new faces in the club that evening and pointed out the butch sitting with the two femmes. *Hey, that was me!*

After Sheresa left the stage, the first performer, Dee Franklin, came out and lip-synched a Queen Latifah song. People were quick to come up and tip her. I never saw so many people comfortable with being who they were in one spot. After the lip synchronizing performers came the male and female dancers, whom everyone was waiting for! That was a totally bi thing! Both male and females danced for whoever had a dollar bill! I got my first lap dance that night from a dancer named "Desire"! Believe me when I say she fit her stage name.

I would come to the Marquette on a weekly basis and become a regular at the bar. The lip synch shows were great, and I would love to see who would do the new hit song! Over the years, the club would offer me, and the gay patrons that weren't afraid to go into the hood, a variety of entertainment. People would drive up from neighboring states just to get a drink from Debbie at the bar, hear DJ Rick, see Big Man at the door, see Anthony Cartwright do his Prince skits, the Labelles, the Franklins, the Alexanders, the late Greg Holiday and Yolanda "The Big Girl Herself" Walker on stage, just to name a few.

I mostly had fun when I came to the club alone. Except for that first night, it was always a disaster when I brought someone I was dating to the Marquette. Nevertheless, the shows made it worth coming every time!

I was always too shy to meet someone at the club, so I would still rely on the chat line and newspaper personals to meet women. I had moved back into the house with mom and Bernard found a place to stay in East Point. My mother never asked me about where I would spend my evenings after work. She was just happy with me being back in the house with my daughters. Junior was doing a lot better in school after I returned to the house, and he became my video game buddy! I started to feel a little happiness! However, it was only the beginning.

I met this woman named Rose that answered one of my newspaper ads. She was a junior at Agnes Scott College. I really enjoyed talking to her on the phone, and it was only a matter of weeks before I went to her dorm to meet her. She was a very sweet young lady, a virgin lesbian, totally untouched by a man— way too good for me at that time! I really didn't deserve her. Rose was beautiful in every way, but I wasn't attracted to her. Beauty is truly in the eye of the beholder, and people who you see as attractive may come over as very unattractive to the next person. What I did wrong is that I started a relationship with her.

Rose was my first real lesbian relationship, although I did not see it as one at the time. We would meet each other and go out, be intimate, and tell each other things that we wouldn't share with other people. I would invite her over to my house and she met my mother, Junior and even Bernard. After a few months, I invited her to accompany Vee, Junior and myself on a trip to the aquarium in Chattanooga. We had loads of fun together. It would only go downhill when I became a total jerk!

I never stopped answering responses to my personals after I started dating Rose. I had no idea that she was slowly falling in love with me. I just thought that we were really enjoying each other's company. I was wrong. I was misleading her into thinking that we were developing a long-term relationship and I would later pay dearly for hurting her.

Chapter 9

A Fool in Love

"Nichelle"
(1995)

By 1995, I was an official gay nightclub hopper! Some great lesbian nightspots like the Library and Revolutions had just closed up when I came out, but I didn't miss all of the party. I had now been turned on to the Otherside on Wednesday nights, as well as Lorettas and Traxx. I had an all week Atlanta nightclub itinerary.

I wasn't only interested in clubbing. I went to Ansley Mall and was greeted by all the races of the rainbow. I started patronizing the community shops and restaurants in the Ansley area, and did most of my gay and lesbian research at Outwrite & Charis Bookstores. I was very happy and excited to finally be myself!

Rose never went with me to the Marquette or any other club. She was heavily into her classes and didn't have much time to actually go out. She wanted to settle down with me for the future and I was trying to break out of a shell! I never pressured her to come out and party with me because I wasn't as serious about our relationship as she was, and I wanted her to keep her focus on school.

I kept answering the same woman's personal ad. Her name was Nichelle and she lived in Cobb County. Her ad said that she was half-Asian and Black and spoke a little Chinese. By now, you can tell that bilingual women intrigue me! I really wanted to meet her and kept sending her messages. After about two weeks, she finally called me. We met each other at the electronics store near Cobb Parkway where she worked. She wasn't at all what I'd expected, but I'd decided that even though there may not be a physical attraction for her, that I would date her because of her great personality.

Nichelle had a calico cat and wanted to be a veterinarian at one time. Just like my dream woman! Remember the movie, *Turner & Hooch*, with Tom Hanks? The vet woman came up to him and initiated the relationship! I love go-getter women like that! I didn't think of Nichelle as my dream woman, but I loved her desire to take care of and nurture animals. We would go to the pound, slip them dog biscuits, and point out all the ones we would rescue if we had our own farm. She gave me the chance of having a life with a woman that cared for others less fortunate than she was. That's the perfect woman for me. Beauty inside and out!

One day we were pumping gas and Nichelle said something beautiful.

"Suppose you were pumping gas and you went in and someone had already paid for it? Wouldn't that be a great thing to do for someone? For a stranger to pay for their gas, or to pay their bills for no reason. I want to be able to do stuff like that someday."

Anyone that knows me personally would understand why that statement would get to me. I love doing random acts of kindness. She didn't have to do or say anything else to have me! I was sprung!

"That's a sweet thing to say, Nichelle. I'd like to do that too if I had the money. I've always said that if I ever hit the lottery I'd rent the Georgia Dome and have all my old neighborhoods come down and pay everyone's rent and utility bills up for the month! Then I'd give them a free concert or something! On the spot!"

We smiled at each other and the rest was history. We were getting married! That's all there was to it! Just one week was all it took! (Actually, if the typical lesbian relationship doesn't have you moving in or at least taking about a future together after the first week—you can forget about it!)

I was young, new to the scene and I had never experienced the beauty of lesbian love. Most women love deep and romance and commitment comes very easy for us. (And so does deceit, but you find that out much later!) Nichelle wrote me a love letter and sprayed it with her favorite perfume. I still have it.

"To my Boo, Love Nichelle.
Here's a letter coming straight from my heart about how much I miss you when we are apart. You came along when no one else could and stole my heart. But you know it's all good. It's only seven whole days and six long nights since I laid eyes on you but you believe that baby I'm so in love with you. So at the closing of this letter all I want to say is that I do love you and want to marry you someday. I didn't forget my baby girls I love them just as much as I do you. I know its short but I am falling asleep and I'm very anxious to see you. I love you. Your future wife, Nichelle."

Romantic and the ability to express her love in spoken word and writing! Nichelle gave me just want I wanted and I was very infatuated.

It got to the point where I had just stopped talking to Rose altogether. She would call and I would let it go to an answering machine, or just let it ring. I didn't mean to have hurt her but I just didn't know what to say. It wasn't just because I wasn't attracted to her. I wasn't physically attracted to Nichelle either. It's just that Nichelle had more of the inside qualities that I was looking for in my mate.

How the heck can you tell someone that they are just not what you are looking for on the inside or outside? That wouldn't be very nice would it? Well, just not speaking to them is not nice either, but that's the choice I made. That's what most idiots do that fall in love with another person while they're dating someone else!

I looked at my relationship with Rose as just dating. I wasn't serious with her, and I never told her that I loved her. When did we get into a romantic relationship anyway? Did it start just because I slept with her? I never wrote her a love note or a poem, and that's when you can tell I really like you! Rose would finally catch me over to my mom's house one evening. I told her about Nichelle and she would say something that would confuse me for over a decade about women.

"When I invited you into my dorm room and welcomed you into my bed we started a romantic relationship! I'm not an easy person. I am a virgin! A real woman doesn't invite you into her bed for nothing! You said that you wanted to start a relationship in your ad and that's why I answered it!"

A real woman doesn't invite you into her bed for nothing.

That philosophy stuck with me after she said it. I felt really bad and apologized. I had no idea that it was that strong of a statement for her to be intimate with me.

After she accepted my apology, she moved in for a kiss. For the record, I don't cheat! Bernard and I had already separated when I was intimate with Sabrina. Once I am in a relationship with you then I am in it faithfully until the end. Since I was in a relationship with Nichelle, I pushed Rose away before she could kiss me. I could really see that she was very hurt after I did, so I left. She remained at the house and talked to my mom while I went to work.

I called my mom after my shift, and told her that Nichelle and I were going to the Marquette. My mom said that Rose was still there! She had waited at my mom's house for me for over an 8-hour shift. I really didn't know what to do! I didn't have to come home because Nichelle had bought us new matching Nike short sets to wear that night to the club.

"Mom, I'm not coming home. I'm going straight to Smyrna to change at Nichelle's house. Tell Rose that—"

She cut me off right there! Mom then made it clear to me that she wasn't my secretary, and that I had to deliver my own messages. Actually, she used the words "dirty work" in there somewhere! I wasn't out to my mom at all, but the way she handled that made me wonder how much she actually knew!

I did tell Rose that I was going out with Nichelle that night. She didn't sound too upset and asked me if I could stop by her college dorm the next day. I told her that I probably wouldn't be able to because I would be too tired. I really liked her, and I didn't want to be a jerk about this situation. I just didn't know how else to handle it.

Bernard would tell me later in life that butches take on manly-like roles, but the key that separates some of us from most heterosexual men is that we care too much about the woman's feelings. *Eh?*

He said that it should not have bothered me as much as it did to have picked Nichelle over Rose. So what? I chose whom I wanted to be with. That's life and Rose will get over it!

Ok? There you have it! One heterosexual man's look on the issue!

That night at the Marquette was a busy one for me. I had some of Rose's friends there watching me, and obviously calling her and giving her play by play on my date. Nichelle and I had to sit on the steps near the bar as the club was always packed to the gills on a Saturday night.

Directly behind Nichelle was another butch that was constantly easing close to her. Nichelle knew that Rose was at my mother's house that night and wasn't happy about it. She had known about Rose from the start, and that I didn't have a relationship with her, but it was something about her staying over to my mothers to see me that made her upset. I just didn't understand what? It would get uglier.

The butch, named T.J., leaned over to Nichelle and asked her if she was dating someone. Nichelle said, "No", even though I was sitting right next to her!

("Karma" meet L.A., L.A. meet "Karma"! If there ever was a doubt that I was very wrong with the way I handled the Rose and Nichelle situation, then it was erased at that moment.)

Nichelle began calling me less and less and I went into a state of depression. I wasn't depressed alone though. I would find out that Rose was hurting too, and it would show in her classwork. She had started skipping classes and staying in her dorm room crying. Her friends were there to offer support and two of them even volunteered to kick my ass for her if that is what she wanted. *Ah, friends!*

I'm glad that she had a support group. I had no one. My mother was raising Junior and helping to raise my girls. She didn't understand my life and I couldn't talk to her. Bernard was my ex-husband and now proclaimed "baby daddy", how could he be of any help? My brothers thought my life was a joke.

I just didn't have the friend support because I was never good at making friends. I had no choice! I had to get Nichelle to feel the same way for me that she did before! I had to win her love back!

(If I had friends then they would have been there to tell me how stupid that choice was!)

I drove over to Nichelle's apartment and knocked. She didn't answer and I went over to look into her car. I was young, ok! I guess I had a stalker moment!

There was a baseball cap in the front passenger seat and some club flyers from gay nightclubs. I had told Nichelle that I wanted to go to this lesbian club called Towers, but I didn't have the information on how to get there. Sure enough, one of the flyers in the car was from Towers. She had gone there the night before with someone else! *Nichelle didn't wear baseball caps.*

I got in my car and drove off. Before I could even reach the expressway, my pager had a new message waiting. I waited until I got home to check the message.

"I saw you outside and you'd better be glad that Nichelle kept me from coming out there to get you. Stay away from her house or we won't even have to call the police. I'll handle it myself."

I never found out who this person was. It wasn't T.J., as I'd find out later. I'm not the clowning, ghetto type of person so I didn't go back over there. I wrote her a letter and mailed it to her with no response. I stayed at home, too depressed to work and lost my job. My mother wasn't happy about that at all! She used to want me to stay there with her. Now, since she had my daughters to play with, she just wanted me to go out and work. With money from Bernard's child support, her disability, side businesses, and me, she was making enough to rent this big three-bedroom house off Campbellton Road. It was nice and I didn't want to lose it for us, so I moped for about two months, and finally went and got another security gig.

Nichelle called me a week after I got my new job and wanted me to see if I could get her a position with the company. Corporate office was in a very tricky spot near the airport, and I knew how to get there on MARTA, but not too well by driving. I ended up taking her in circles and she got frustrated. I wanted to make her happy and would do anything at that point. I was totally either in love with her, or totally in love with the idea that she was at one time in love with me. *If any of that makes since.*

The talk escalated into an argument about whether or not we would be together again. I really didn't even know how or when we broke up. I asked her how she felt about me.

"You are nice and all that, but remember that you are only the first woman that I have tried to have a relationship with. You are a butch and you know that! I am unclassified! I don't want to be limited to date a butch. I want to date whomever I want and whenever I want! I'm single and I am happy being single!

I just didn't understand or want to believe it! She wrote me this beautiful love letter and said all of these great things to me.

"But Nichelle, you wrote me this letter and told me that you wanted to be with me!" I was really breaking down in her passenger seat.

"That was back in tha day! That's old! I don't want you now and I didn't want you then!"

Back in tha day? That letter was less than 2 months old! I had no idea why it was coming down to this. I had fallen in love, and was now being tossed to the side. I had been deceived! I couldn't think. I became very irrational. For the first time in my life, I lost myself and wanted out! Not just of her car, but out of life itself!

I looked into her rear view passenger mirror and saw a truck just behind us. It would be my way out. I opened her door, and while the car was still in motion, I jumped out of the car unto the path of the truck. We were on Norman Berry Drive just in front of that Dairy Queen across from Tri-Cities High. I still have some of the road impressions and a bruise on my back to this day. My attempted suicide had failed because the truck was too far away.

(OBJECTS IN MIRROR ARE CLOSER THAN THEY APPEAR. Yeah, right! The passenger mirror had obviously deceived me, too!)

The driver of the truck got out and called the police. Even though I was lying face down on the asphalt, I was still conscious. It seemed the driver was really shaken up about seeing me coming out of that car in his path and having to slam on those brakes. I sometimes say a prayer of apology for the trauma I may have caused him. Nichelle was more pissed off then concerned because at first glance it would look like she pushed me out of the car instead of me jumping. I was taken to South Fulton Medical Center where the first words out of the emergency room doctor's mouth were, "It's just not your time yet!"

The next doctor I saw was the mandatory psychiatrist you have to see when you've done something very irrational. He asked me why I wanted to kill myself just two days before my twenty-fifth birthday. Then, we joked about me wanting to get something to eat at Diary Queen, which is why I jumped out right then! He said that my behavior was a sign of bipolar disorder since I was so intelligent about the whole ordeal, and even put it in perspective for him.

The doctor made me an appointment at the mental health clinic and put me on Paxil. I went to the clinic and they didn't accept my HMO. *Figures!*

I came home from work a month later to find Nichelle and her friend Erin in my driveway. That was a shock since Nichelle said she didn't want to have anything else to do with me after the accident. Erin was a White butch from Carrollton. I knew that Erin liked Nichelle and was always suspicious of them, but at that time, I was just happy to see Nichelle again.

During the time that I was away from Nichelle, I had decided that I would go back to school in Savannah. The security company I worked for had a job in nearby Pooler, Georgia and I could work, go to school, and send money back to my mom for the girls. I told them about the trip I had to make to Savannah for registration and that it would be a four-hour drive alone. Nichelle volunteered to drive me down there and Erin would follow us in her new red Camaro.

The day of the drive to Savannah, I met Nichelle and left my car over to her apartment. We then started the ride down South with me in her car and Erin following. I tried to make conversation with Nichelle, and to talk to her about us, but she would ignore any talk of us getting back together. I also noticed that there was a love message from T.J. on the dashboard.

You know those little black suction memo holders? The message was on the second sheet and you could only read it when the wind blew up the paper. During a gas stop, when I returned to the car, Nichelle had propped the first paper where the message was very visible for me to read without the wind. She was clearly messing with my head. She knew that it would bother me.

We had already passed Macon and I was a passenger without a car. I was stuck here and didn't know what to do. I had saved enough for our hotel room and to take Nichelle to Club One that night. We arrived in Savannah and I paid for the room. I tried to flirt with Nichelle and she pushed me off and asked for some beer.

Well, so much for the woman that wanted to do random acts of kindness and save animals a few months ago! This chic wanted some beer! Erin and I got into her car to search Savannah for a liquor store. She tried to make it look like she was in my corner.

"I'm just going to be honest with you, L.A. If she doesn't pick me, than I hope it's you, because I can't stand that damn T.J.! Whenever you are away all she does is talk about is you, so all you have to do is hang in there and make as if you don't want her. She'll want you even more then."

Why does it have to be a game? Why couldn't she just want me? What could she want about me anyway? Didn't I just try to attempt suicide from her car the month before? I guess I should have asked myself those questions before I had them drive me that far away from home. Again, I was young and stupid!

I brought the beer back and we had a few drinks before we went to the club. Nichelle didn't have a good time because no one came up to her so that she could make me jealous more. I guess I was just an ant that she wanted to put a magnifying glass over in the sun and see what would happen. Erin didn't go with us to the club and stayed at the hotel room. I would find out that she would be using the phone calling her girlfriend long distance the whole time running up the hotel bill.

When we got back to the room, Nichelle checked her pager messages and was upset that no one had called her. I went to take a shower and could hear them in the front room laughing. I started to cry. I didn't know what to do, and I didn't understand why she wanted to drive me to Savannah if she didn't want to patch things up between us. I came out of the shower and they stopped laughing. That's a sure sign that they were laughing at the person that was out of the room. Nichelle went in to take her shower. I left her side of the bed uncovered, said good night to Erin, and fell fast asleep before I knew it. I was dead tired and emotionally drained.

I woke up in the middle of the night and saw that Nichelle's side of the bed was still uncovered. I turned over and she was sleeping in the bed with Erin instead of me. I went into the bathroom and drunk beers and cried the rest of the night, which is never a good thing in a situation like that. I had a lot to say when they woke up the next morning! I quickly asked Nichelle why she would even come here with me knowing how I felt about her.

"I just wanted to get a break. I didn't come down here to be with you! I already got somebody and they went out of town with their family! I just wanted to do something to kill time while they were gone!"

I went up to her and she pushed me away. I'm not a violent person. I was only trying to get closer to her to talk. After she pushed me, Erin grabbed me around the neck and forced my head into the floor. Nichelle pulled Erin off me and said that she wasn't going to jail for anyone, and that if we started fighting then the hotel would call the police. I got up and went outside. I needed some air and it was time for my orientation at Savannah Tech. Before I left the parking lot, Nichelle ran out of the room.

"If you touch my car then I'll kill you!" she said.

I just shook my head in disgust. I'm not that type of person no matter what I'm faced with. Then Erin yelled out the same thing. "If she touches my car I'll kill her. She won't have to try to kill herself again! I'll do it for her!"

I walked to Savannah Tech and went to the orientation. It turned out that I wouldn't have enough money to attend classes even if I took the job in Pooler. I had defaulted on my Pell grant and owed GSU, so I couldn't get another grant.

When I got back to the hotel, both Nichelle and Erin were long gone in their cars, and left me penniless and without a ride to get back to Atlanta. I went to the office to see if I could get my night deposit back and that's when I found out about Erin and the long distance phone calls! I couldn't get my deposit, I couldn't stay another night in the room, and to set the stage even better, it was pouring raining in Savannah as it does most of the time!

I walked across the street to a nearby strip mall and asked some people how far it was to the downtown area, and to the Greyhound bus station. I was crying and most people walked away without even saying a word. I stopped asking after the third person ignored me and sat down in the grass on the side of a store in the rain.

I've never mentioned my faith or beliefs in this book so far, but I want to tell you now that I've always believed in angels and good people. I've had plenty come and give me hope at the darkest of times. That day in Savannah, when I was stranded far from home with no money, a woman walked up and gave me a bus pass without me asking her. She said that she had an extra one and told me how to get to the Greyhound bus station. It just happened to be on the same bus line where I already was. I said thank you and she just smiled and walked back over to the curb.

When the bus came, everyone got on it except for the woman that gave me her bus pass. She walked into a store in the strip mall and disappeared. She had been standing at that bus stop when I crossed the street with the other people, and waited there the whole time for the bus—even after she gave me the pass. Then she just didn't get on! I looked to see if there was someone with her. There wasn't anyone that she was talking to, or waiting for, or anything like that. I stopped crying, because I knew then that somehow God would get me home unharmed.

I called Bernard when I got to the bus station and he and my mother wired the money to get me on a bus back to Atlanta. Nichelle had called my mother and told her that I had too much to drink and had gone ballistic on her and Erin! *You have got to be kidding me!*

My mom said that she didn't believe a word of it, but she knew that they had my car. Nichelle promised her to drive it back to my house, so she *apologized* for my behavior to keep the peace, and to get my car back.

I got back to Atlanta around 10:00 PM and rode the MARTA bus home. I was exhausted. I kissed my mom and the girls, and called Bernard to thank him. I had been out in the rain and on a cold Greyhound bus for 7 hours and had caught a nasty cold.

I settled into bed a few hours later when I heard my car pull into the driveway with the red Camaro behind it. I watched Nichelle and T.J. get out of my car and leave my keys in the mailbox. They both then got into the car with Erin and drove off. I took a dose of NyQuil and went to sleep.

I had to work overtime hours to pay back Bernard and my mom for that bus ticket, but was excited when I got it done, and even gave them a little extra just for being there. We were having more problems at home with Junior. He had been running with some of the neighborhood boys and was hooked on speed. Mom had to call the police on him one day while I was at work and they had to get him off the roof of someone's house. He had become too much for her to take care of and he went to live with his other grandmother. I suggested to mom that we move to a smaller place again to save money now that he had moved out.

Just before we moved, I got a pager message from T.J. She sent it at about 2:00 AM. I could distinguish it from the first person's voice and knew it wasn't the same. The message stated that Nichelle was very happy with her and that all of her ex-girlfriends can forget about dating her again!

Well, considering the fact that she was the cause of severe emotional trauma, left me stranded in Savannah, and I hadn't called her in weeks, then I don't think that message was even necessary!

(I wasn't completely through with Nichelle, though and her story didn't end here)

After the "stay away from Nichelle" call from T.J., I decided that I needed to find someone to ease the pain from losing her. I knew what I wanted and she had given it to me for the briefest of moments. I was on a search for romance. I wouldn't care about being attracted to the woman. Maybe I can look inside these women, romance them, and fulfill their deepest desires. Who knows, maybe I can even find happiness with that special one!

My mother cleaned out her attic during that move and I found an old Royal Traveler briefcase that one of her borders left back in the seventies. I placed Nichelle's love letter to me in the briefcase in a plastic bag so I could still smell the perfume. I didn't know it at that time, but that briefcase would hold memories from passing events from then on. I still have it in my possession, and it contains some of the most important moments of my life, including mementos from the women that would cross my path over the next ten years.

(I remember these times in "The Briefcase Files")

Chapter 10

The Briefcase Files Part I

"Bridgett"
(1996)

I started to read the local gay and lesbian newspaper, Southern Voice, and decided to place an ad in their personals. It's a totally 1-900 voice mail system now, but back then, they use to let you place an ad and put in a post office box for responses.

"SBF, 25, 5'10, sexy, athletic, romantic butch seeking feminine female, 18-24, that loves children, animals and looking for romance. Mail responses to..."

I think that was little better than my first one, don't you? I had learned a lot about who I was, and what I was looking for. I got a response from this woman named Bridgett in Decatur first!

3/29/96
"Dear 5'10, Athletic, Sexy, Romantic, etc,
I saw your ad in the Southern Voice and it captured my attention. I like the words that you used to describe yourself—especially the "R" word. What was it again? Rough, ready, reckless? Ah, no—it was romantic! I absolutely adore the art of romance—and it is an art form! (smiley face).
As for me—I'm 5'4, 110ibs, with a dancer's build... I will use the "P" word to describe myself! I know what you are thinking—but let's not jump the gun. The "P" word is passionate, because I believe that passion is the height of life. Those things that one does best are those that they feel most passionate about and I aim to be passionate in all my endeavors! Call me 770-....."

Ok. She sounds interesting enough. She did own her own business and was quite attractive. I would take her out on one date. I went to pick her up at her house in Decatur, which was quite large! I would find out later that she was married and that was her *and* her husband's house! We went to Boccaccio, this Italian restaurant that used to be downtown, and we might as well had gone to McDonalds, because when I say that Bridgett had to have it "her way"—it definitely had to be that!

"Excuse me, this glass is too dirty and her, (referring to me), setting is wrong. She has two salad forks."

For the record, I wasn't even going to have a salad! Bridgett also wasted no time cutting to her most pressing question she had for me.

"So, why do you dress like a man? Haven't you ever heard of a soft butch? Why don't try that for a change?"

Ok, it was my clothes again. I like men's clothing! I've always have! It's only a part of what makes me. I had heard the term *soft butch*, but never thought about it referring to me, or even changing myself to become one. I never even knew what I could do to change myself into one, at least not until Bridgett kept talking...

"Ok, so how about a dress?" I shook my head no. "Ok. What is wrong with a dress? Is it uncomfortable for you to wear one? I didn't like them either when I was younger because I could never find one that was comfortable enough for me. Maybe that's it with you. You just need to find one that fits you comfortably!"

The waiter returned with a new glass of water and my salad fork and I think he was really trying to get away before Bridgett noticed that he had returned, but...

"Do you have lemons? I thought you would give us lemons with this water. Can I have some lemons, please? And, we are having the Caesar salad with some extra croutons for me. Give us about ten or fifteen more minutes to decide on the entrée."

The next hour I would learn how bad of an example I was setting for the gay community by being such a hard butch. How if I was going to wear a striped suit then I should wear a solid tie, and how she still runs the household as a strong lesbian even though her husband remained after she came out! She even asked me to come in so that *he* could fix me some coffee. I passed.

(The original letter above is in the briefcase from Bridgett!)

Nichelle came back into the picture for a brief moment as I was asked to accompany her to pick up her boyfriend from jail. Yes, her boyfriend! Women were apparently out of the picture for a minute as she had a new apartment and a new man!

I was stopped in Cobb County by police for a wobbly car tag and a cracked windshield. Unfortunately, I had also left my new insurance card at the house! I got a ticket on the way to the jail, to help my ex-girlfriend's new boyfriend get out of jail! *Bummer!*

"Joy"
(1996)

I went back to the chat line this time and met a woman from Griffin, GA. She said she was in her twenties and that she had a daughter. I had just purchased a new Camry and made the drive to Griffin to meet her. She lived in the poorest section of the city in a project-like apartment complex. I sat down on her couch and colored with her toddler daughter. In the midst of coloring, a huge brown cockroach ran across the book, and I went outside of the lines to smack it away. Her daughter was mostly mad because I messed up her picture, and wasn't even concerned by the cockroach!

I wasn't comfortable, and I knew this wasn't going to work, but Joy was a very sweet girl. I was attracted to her because of her story of abuse from her ex-boyfriend. It was the damsel in distress thing again! She wanted to leave Griffin, move to Atlanta with her daughter, and start a new life. I thought it would be perfect, so we kept talking.

One weekend I drove her up to Atlanta and we stayed in the Comfort Inn. She said that she had never been romanced before, so I really went all out for her. Roses in the room, a bottle of wine and some fresh fruit! I even bought her some books to read for when she returned home including, *How Stella Got Her Groove Back.*

It didn't matter as she had already read the book anyway! It sparked a conversation between us about age difference and romance. She asked me how old would the youngest woman be that I would date. I was 26 at the time so I told her 18. I asked her why and she didn't answer me—but kissed me!

In fact, after that she said nothing for about two hours, as we would enjoy the hotel room and each other's company. *(You know what I mean! I hope some of you are not reading this book for too much lesbian erotica. This is my life story for Pete's sake! Some of you even know me. I'm not going to get too raunchy with the details!)*

Afterwards, we held each other and she said that she needed to tell me something. She had already mentioned the abuse and that she had to have a special operation in order to have her daughter. I asked her what it was, and she tried to kiss me again. I stopped her and told her that distracting me wouldn't work a second time, and that she could trust me with whatever she needed to tell me. She took a deep breath before she told me and I found out why!

"I had the operation because I'm not 23. I'm actually 14 years old."

Ok. So, underage teenage girl and wine in a single occupancy hotel room. I had just committed several Georgia felonies! She said she was 23. Her ad said that she was 23! Heck, she *looked* 23! I'm not in the habit of asking the women that I date to see their drivers licenses or anything!

She had a daughter that had to be at least 3 or 4 years old! On the other hand, was that even her daughter? At that point, all I wanted to do was get her out of that hotel room and back home! I got her down highway 19/41 extremely fast!

(The Comfort Inn Hotel bill is in the briefcase!)

The 1996 Summer Olympic Games in Atlanta would not be forgotten either. I still didn't have a girlfriend. On top of that, I could only get a ticket for the Water Polo event at Georgia Tech, which Bernard and I attended. We did see the U.S. men win a match! I wanted a ticket to the Opening Ceremonies, but I ended up having to watch them from the Forsyth Street Bridge. The U.S. Army fighter jets and the fireworks display flying over Olympic Stadium during the national anthem was a sight to remember! It was one of the only times that I really caught a patriotic chill!

I hadn't heard anything from Nichelle and didn't have a way to contact her. I had also missed my court date for that ticket in Cobb County and that wasn't a good at all!

Mom was watching the girls one evening and I went to Centennial Olympic park to get away. I watched several free bands perform that evening and the entire first set of Jack Mack and the Heart Attacks. I sat by that crazy looking statue in the park that looks like half a sundial with people stuck running in it for almost three hours just listening to the music.

The Olympic free concert itinerary on the guardrail read that LadySmith Black Mambazo would also be performing that week, and I decided to come back to the Park to see them. I loved their African dance songs! Jack Mack said that they would be coming back to play until 2 AM, and I wanted to hear them again because they did a great rendition of the Staple Singer's *"I'll Take You There"*. After being in the park in that same spot for hours, I left during their break to find a telephone.

As I was coming out of the park at the Luckie Street entrance about 20 uniformed police officers passed me running into the section where I had been sitting. I noticed them, but really paid them no attention. During the Olympics, there were thousands of people downtown and the streets looked like a never ending Peachtree Road Race! I just thought they were doing crowd control.

I went to a phone and called Bernard to let him and mom know where I was. I heard the band start to play again and was trying to get off the phone with him to go back to the park. He talked to me longer than I really wanted him to. Finally, I just told him to tell my mom I would be home soon.

I hung up the phone and was just a few yards away from the Luckie Street park entrance when I heard a loud boom! I looked up and saw smoke rising right in front of me in the area of the park where I was walking, and white debris flying everywhere! It was from one of the big white speaker towers, and I just thought it malfunctioned or something.

Then a guy came running and yelling to the street vendors that it was a bomb and to pack everything up! People were screaming and running and police were yelling, "Clear the streets!", "Clear the streets!"

I ran all the way home from Luckie Street to Peachtree Street to Forsyth Street, across the Castleberry bridge, down Fair Street, and then down Westview Drive where we lived. Nonstop! No joke! If you don't live in Atlanta, or don't know of those streets, then let's just say that it was a very, very _long_ sprint!

I probably racked up about ten gold medals for the U.S. in that run alone! I was scared and totally pissed off that someone set off a bomb in my hometown! Ladysmith wouldn't get to perform as planned, because they closed the Park after the Centennial Park bombing.

Over 100 people were injured and one woman was killed from that horrible sound I heard. Looking in the Atlanta Journal-Constitution newspaper that next day, I would see dozens of people lying hurt near that crazy statue that I was sitting by for 3 hours, and just happened to walk away from only 15-20 minutes before the explosion. I left because Jack Mack had stopped playing and I had to call my mother. A moment where God again moved me just seconds out of harms way and I am very grateful.

(The water polo ticket and other 1996 items are in the briefcase)

I was finally able to buy my first computer during the end of 1996, and quickly turned to online dating. In the lesbian Sistah's chat room, I met up with Nichelle again. She was staying in a hotel room in Decatur with her new extremely violent girlfriend. We had been away from each other for almost a year, and she had tattoos and piercings now. I went to the hotel room to see her and she told me that her mother had finally moved to Georgia, and that she was moving in with her and her aunt.

I was there to assist with the move, and met her mother for the first time. She didn't like me because she was already attached to the abusive girl her daughter was dating. I was totally pissed! This woman did not care that even after what her daughter had done to me, I would still try to help her on occasion.

That night the girlfriend went totally nuts and threw all of Nichelle's clothes into the hotel parking lot. She called me and I got out of bed to help her take the stuff to her aunt's house. Her mother was somewhat happy, but still didn't take a liking to me. I was out of there!

Nichelle's mother was terminally ill and actually died the first of that next year. I offered my condolences. She asked for money to buy something to wear to her mom's funeral. I wasn't working at the time and had nothing. I asked my mother and Bernard if they wanted to pitch in.

(Ok? Probably not the best folks to ask for a donation since they were the ones that had to help when she left me stranded in Savannah, ya think?)

They totally said no! I thought long and hard about it. I was really in love with this woman at one time. My mom came into my room and put her arms around me.

"Lisa, it's alright to care for someone and want to help, but this girl obviously cared nothing about you when she left you stranded and her mother didn't even like you. Just give your condolences and that's all."

I listened to my mother that time. I had done more than enough, and I couldn't help anymore. I lost touch with her again.

"Regina"
(1997)

A found another chat line with a section for women seeking women called Telepersonals. It was free for women to meet men, but if you wanted to talk to women, regardless of what sex you were—you had to pay for response time. It wasn't that much, and their office was right downtown so I went and paid enough to answer a few personal ads.

One of them was a woman named Regina that lived in a rough area near the Federal Penitentiary. Of course, I didn't know that until I got there!

I parked outside of her apartment and she came out to meet me. I gave her a bottle of Sutter Home and she kissed me and invited me in. She had a couple of daughters and lived with this man. Of course, I didn't know that either! She said that the guy was her distant cousin, and that they used to fool around at one time. He needed a place to stay so she hooked him up at her place. He and her daughters had gone to movies, but she said that I would get a chance to meet them later. That's good, but I couldn't resist, and just had to ask her.

"So, is he the father of your daughters?"

She got upset and I don't know why. You admitted that the two of you used to fool around, so I thought it would be all right to ask. You have given me too much information to begin with! I just thought you would feel like sharing more!

She told me that he wasn't, but that *he* claimed that he was for the youngest one. I said ok. I then asked her if I could have a drink of the wine that I had just brought her. I was suddenly feeling queasy!

She pointed me in the direction of the kitchen to find a corkscrew. I popped open the white zinfandel like a lush and poured it into a tall plastic cup as if it was Kool-Aid! No room for etiquette here!

While I was satisfying my thirst, someone began banging at her door and yelling. I could see the silhouette of a tall man standing outside her apartment. He was demanding to know where her distant cousin was! She started yelling back and the man pulled out a gun! He stuck it her face through the screen! I couldn't get to her back door without the man seeing me, so I deemed it best to duck down beside the refrigerator. I started praying and gulping down the wine at the same time!

The arguing suddenly stopped and the two of them burst into laughter! They both came into the kitchen and pointed to me on the floor with the wine bottle in my lap! It was her neighbor that had the gun and they were just fooling around to scare me.

Well, it worked and I wasn't amused at all!

"You said that you like to protect your girlfriends, so I was waiting on you to come in and rescue me!" Regina was laughing to tears as she introduced me to her neighbor.

For her information, she wasn't my girlfriend! Even if she was, I don't think I was coming in there to rescue her from a gangsta! I was hoping that he would just shoot her, run away and not had noticed me in the kitchen! I had already planned that I would run out the back after I heard her body hit the floor!

They had their laugh, and we even talked for a little while, but I certainly wasn't feeling anything that night! I saw my chance to leave when they both complained that I didn't leave them any of the wine.

"I'll go to the store and get some more. Sorry I didn't leave any, but you two scared the hell out of me!"

Regina put her arms around me and kissed me. She said that she was sorry, and would ride with me to the store, but that I had to buy the wine because she was only 19. *When would I start asking these women to see their ID?*

For the record, she was a great kisser, but I told her that I would go alone and bring the wine back. I got in my car and while reaching for my keys, I saw that I had a cork in my pocket. It was from the Sutter Home I drank while in fear for my life.

Did I go to the liquor store and come back? Would you have? I went straight home and got the briefcase out of my closet.

(The Sutter Home cork is in the briefcase to remind me of Regina)

I met a stud that I would try to become friends with at the Otherside one Wednesday night. I don't recall her name, but I told her about Nichelle, and the incident with Regina that had just happened.

"L.A., you have several things that you are doing wrong here! For one, all of the women that you have ever met and tried to start something with have come from chat lines and personals! Those women have problems! That Regina and her neighbor just used you for a good laugh! She knew you weren't coming back from that liquor store! You told her over the phone that you like to protect your women. She saw that as a joke and wanted to make a fool out of you! She was mean and a loser--just like all chat line women!"

I put in my argument in that it's hard to meet single women at clubs, and that some women don't go out much, so personal ads are their way to connect with people! Besides, I'm a good, normal lesbian without a problem, and I use the personals! She wasn't buying it.

"None of that is true, L.A. If a woman has all of the qualities that you are looking for, then she is not going to be in the personals. She is already dating, or is single and waiting for you to cross her path. She doesn't even look at the personals because she has friends that hook her up, or she goes to gay events and is introduced to women there! She's not going to read about you in a paper personal ad or hear your voice on a chat line!" At this point, I was only half-listening, but she continued,

"You said you want a woman that wants a relationship, that is intelligent, speaks another language, diverse and cares about others. Do you really think that you will find that woman on a chat line? Chat lines and personals are for people who are looking for sex and suckers!"

I didn't respond to her, and didn't even want to acknowledge that she made any sense at all. I still wanted to believe that I would find the right woman for me the way I was going about it. We were with two other studs that night and they returned to our table, I quickly wanted to change the talk subject. However, before I could, she finished her point.

"Oh, and by the way, you *do* have several problems. One is that you are on those chat lines trying to find that woman that will never be on there! Second, is that you are letting the women that you do find on there use you because you are trying to be their hero. You are hoping that they will fall for you if you treat them right. It doesn't work that way, L.A. They won't fall for you. They will keep using you, and finally lose all respect for you, and throw you away! You are too good of a person to let these women use you. I hope will see that soon."

I got so angry at this stud that night that I never spoke to her again and even forgot her name. How could she tell me that I had a problem? She didn't have anyone in her life either! What did she know?

Sorry, I was never good at sarcasm. I know that she told me the truth that night, but I just wasn't hearing it.

"Tamela"
(1997)

The black lesbian community in Atlanta is only so big, and it was getter smaller every year I was out! Nine times out of ten, you will cross paths with someone that dated your ex-girlfriend or knew someone that did. I was already concerned about this woman named Tamela after we found out that we both had dated Nichelle. I listened to her voice to see if she was that mystery woman that left me that voice message not to come back to Nichelle's house two years ago.

She wasn't, but she told me that she knew who it was. I found out that Nichelle had two or three suitors at the same time she was conspiring with me, and that Tamela was the one that had gone out of town with her family while she was in Savannah with me.

Things with Tamela didn't progress at all as she was being heavily chased by a woman she didn't want, (who would turn out to be an ex-girlfriend of both Rose *and* Lynda!), and was in love with another woman, (who at that time would be dating a woman that I would meet later on!) I met Tamela's mother, her children and her ex-husband, whom she lived with at the time!

I just couldn't escape the lesbian that still lived with her ex-husband back in those days! When I came out, I moved away from mine, but obviously, the norm was to keep him hanging around!

We would spend time together, but never kissed or crossed the lines to a relationship or intimacy. I had cut communication with her because we just weren't going anywhere and she wrote me this letter:

5/13/97
L.A., first off I really like you a lot. Boo, you are so damn special to me, but somehow you seem to think that I don't give a crap. Baby that is not true at all, okay. When I told you that I wanted us to get to know each other better this was for our own good. I didn't want us to be a one night stand or just a quick fuck between

the two of us because I like you from the first time we met. Boo, couldn't you respect me more for wanting this? Because good things come to those who wait right? Anyway these like few weeks have been really great between us. You've showed me a really great time and I will return the fun as soon as I get back on the rite track. L.A. please don't give up on us because there's a very brite lite at the end of the tunnel. I'm really in a bind rite now and really can't concentrate on this relationship because I am worried about losing everything I have in storage and how I'm going to get the money up. Baby, I put a smile on my face every day but inside I am dying with worration. I am really tired of feeling this way, baby. L.A., I really enjoy you honey cup so much so don't think anything less. And as for your kids I really love the little pumpkins too they are so sweet and we will all spend family time together as soon as I get this problem solved because I am going crazy thinking about this date and nite. Love you, Tamela.

Well two things after she wrote that letter were certain. I realized that Tamela needed money, and that she had no idea how to use "ight" to spell the words "light", "right" and "night". Is "worration" even a word?

Before you say that I'm being a jackass--I paid the cost to be a one and poke fun at that letter now, because I believed every word of that back then and gave Tamela the $200 that she said she needed to keep her storage. I only saw her a few times after I gave her the money. We were still never intimate and she didn't return my phone calls for over a week. Finally, I got a voice message one evening.

Hello L.A. I'm just calling all of my "friends" to let them know that (ex-girl's name) and I'm moving out West to start a new life and wanted to say goodbye to all of you before we left.

Now I was pissed off! I wasn't crying or upset about this one! Just flat out lesbian pissed the fuck off! I called her and told her that I don't care where she was moving with this woman that it would never ever work because she was a lying, no good...*you get the picture!*

Some months later, she even had the nerve to send me another message about how she wished I could see how beautiful the mountains were out West. I had told her I wanted to travel there and she was just rubbing it in. She ended the message saying that she missed me. *(Of all the shuck and jive!)* I hurried and changed my phone number.

I would see her children later on and even her and the woman together back in Georgia! We never spoke again. I even looked her right in the eye at Wal-Mart one day, and she pretended she didn't see me and walked away. Oh well, not as if we had anything to talk about!

(The letter above is in the briefcase to remind me of Tamela)

"Fox"
(1997)

I was still a regular at the Marquette Club on Saturday night. You could hardly find a date there because it was generally a coupled up thing. If you approached someone you would almost definitely be in for a fight if they did have someone, even if you apologized afterwards!

For that reason, I continued to stick with the personal ads. I went one Saturday night to meet a woman that answered my ad. She said that she was a dancer there every now and then. She described herself and we arranged for her to meet me at the bar. I would be holding a $5.00 tip for her.

Fox already lived with a male-female couple. The woman was bisexual and the husband was ok with it, and even allowed Fox to live there with them. That was an interesting living and sleeping arrangement. The story didn't stop there. Fox was also dating a stud outside of their relationship, and the woman didn't know about it! Where would I fit into all of this? Fox said that she didn't know, but she found me quite attractive and wanted to be intimate with me.

I would meet her at the Comfort Inn and would treat her to an evening of romance and lust! *Mostly lust!*

How could I ever be seriously romantic with someone that had two other relationships going on? She was sweet and admitted that her heart was with the other stud that she was dating. She had just wanted to have some fun with me, but she could see that I wanted more than she obviously could give. I wished her the best after our night together, and hoped that she would find happiness with one of them.

(The Comfort Inn hotel bill is in the briefcase to remind me of Fox)

In 1997, I would get a position in customer service at Telepersonals, the very same chat line that I met the woman I had dated. It would be the best job I would ever have because most of the staff was homosexual. The same company that owned Telepersonals also owned Manline and Womanline personals and they were based out of Canada. I would be the only out lesbian on staff with about five or six homosexual males! Our supervisor and a few other staff members were heterosexual and we would sometimes clash, but the majority of the time we would get along.

Being a staff member meant that I had free response time and could respond to any personal ad I wanted to! I looked up my old account and saw that in the past two years I had spent over $200 with the company. Now that my responses were free, and I got the chance to hear all the ads even before they even went online, I didn't want to answer them anymore. *Figures!*

Some of my ex-dates found out that I worked for the line and would call into customer service and ask for free time to respond to ads and check messages. Since that was tracked and deducted from my salary, I said no to most of them.

I had worked for Telepersonals for about two months when Nichelle called in and said that she had a few messages in her mailbox. She asked how my mom, the girls and I were doing and if I was seeing anyone.

Oh, no! I wasn't going to go through anything else with her! It was beyond time to close her chapter! I told her that all were fine, and that I was still single. I then offered to give her enough time to check her messages. She took the free response time and said thank you before hanging up. I never heard from Nichelle again, but I felt at that moment that we had closure, and all was forgiven.

(My job offer letter from Telepersonals is in the briefcase)

My mother's Medicaid benefits would change and for the first time in twenty years as she was assigned a new doctor. This doctor would take her off the Vasotec high blood pressure medication she had been taking for over a decade, and give her another brand. I always questioned this change because my mother's health slowly began to deteriorate afterwards.

She would need my assistance more and more at home, as she wouldn't be able to maintain her household and the children as before. She totally resisted help and would demand that I just keep giving her money, and that she could still handle the house. It was the beginning of a huge power struggle between the two of us to keep things in order.

"Veronica"
(1998)

I met Veronica when she answered my ad on Telepersonals. She lived in Missouri and was moving to Atlanta later that year. She had three children and didn't live with her ex-husband or anything like that, so I was excited about talking to her. She did have some problems with coming out to her family and that was the reason for the move. We talked for long hours every evening and were really getting close.

I have another desire to move a woman into Atlanta and give her a tour! I'm high on my hometown and couldn't wait to show her and her kids the city since they had never been here. She sent me this letter just before she moved.

8/17/98
Hello You!

Here are the pictures I promised you! There aren't as good as I would like them to have been because of the background, but hold on to them and when we see each other I will ex-change these for better ones! L.A. it is getting hard for me to maintain my feelings for you.

There is so much going through my head where you are concerned and it scares me...but I like what I'm feeling. It's like, as long as you're on my mind nothing can bother me...nothing can harm me. All I want to know if what kind of spell you have put on me! I truly adore you and I just can't wait to melt in your arms. I truly believe that fate wants us together!! Miss You. Your baby-boo Ms. Veronica. (smiley face) XOXO.

  I would find out later that Veronica had sent a letter asking me to send some money to Missouri to help her move. I had lost the post office box that she was writing to and never got that letter. She had already changed her phone number and I couldn't contact her. Since we lost contact, I thought that she had brushed me off. She still had my work number and did not call me. It was about a week or two later after we lost contact when she finally called me at work—from Georgia! She was already in town!

  She said that she was so happy! She had met up with her ex-girlfriend and that they had fallen back in love with each other and were moving to Atlanta together. She said that she got mad because I didn't answer her letter and said that I was full of crap!

  I just happen to lose contact for a few days because you were moving and disconnected your phone, and *I'm* full of crap! I was so upset that I slammed the phone down on her!

  I never met her in person, but I still have the pictures she sent and I think that I've seen her around town in some clubs. I think I dodged a bullet from a woman that wanted to use me that time. You two instantly fall back in love and decide to relocate together in a week? I think those two had planned this and I was supposed to help pay for trip! I bet the girl even took the pictures because one of them was of Veronica half-naked!

(The letter is in the briefcase to remind me of Veronica)

Still going solo. December 19, 2006.

December 19, 2006
6:32 PM
Lithonia, GA USA
(Location: My Writing Closet)

I think I'll take a present day break here. It's been too cold to go by the lake to write, so I've made up a writing section in my bedroom closet. I'm sitting in here now beside my clothes and typing on a desktop that I've crammed in this small space. Am I still in pain? You bet! That's why I'm still writing!

So far, I've told you about my childhood, my problems with hiding my sexuality in school and work, my heterosexual common law marriage, my children, coming out lesbian and even my relationship with Nichelle, the first person I ever fell in love with. There would be another, but you'll read about her later.

In case you are wondering, I changed the name of everyone in the book I met starting in high school to protect their privacy. I may use names that are similar, and in some cases, if I know them, their middle name instead of their first. I don't want to embarrass anyone so if you tell someone that you are that person that I am referring to in this book, then it's on you!

How am I right now? I'm doing so-so. I'm still disappointed. I haven't talked to anyone, including that lady that I was dating, in over a week. Yes, I have cut myself off from the world to write this. I have pulled my phone jack out of the wall and I'm on a computer without Internet access. I think I have about 2,000 emails in my Inbox. It's important for me to finish this before the beginning of the New Year.

-- L.A. JohnTre

Chapter 11

The Briefcase Files Part II

"London"
(1998)

There is always a year in one's younger life that they remember as the one where they were most promiscuous. For me, that year would be 1998. I had already been disappointed in the middle of the year by Veronica's attempted deception. It was time for me to have some fun and take a break from finding my future wife. Besides, everyone needs an ego boost every now and then!

I met London from Telepersonals. She was in town from Chicago and just wanted to spend some time with a butch. After a few conversations, we met at the Hampton Inn where I used to work. I had an ex co-worker hook me up with a room key that she hadn't marked as clean, and London and I spent the night in the room.

She was heavy into the role playing thing. By that time, I had become a *packing* butch, (That means that I wear a male attachment during intercourse.) London would have made a heterosexual man very happy with the way she carries on in the bedroom!

"Oh, you are so big! I've never had anything like this! You are the best!"

She was so noisy that I was worried that someone would come to the door—since this *was* a *borrowed* room! I quickly threw a pillow over her mouth! I was laughing most of the time! You'd swear that she was making a porno movie or something! She talked the whole time! I would feel sorry for any man that had sex with her, and she dumped him later and told him that she was faking it! He would have felt really bad!

(The Hampton Inn hotel key is in the briefcase to remind me of London! Not that I needed anything to remember her!)

"Debra"
(1998)

Here's where I taper off in preference a little. Most guys and butches drool for a woman with large size features. I have never been a big breast or big behind lover type. In fact, I'm more attracted to women with smaller features. I would get way much more than that in Debra! She was a 42DDD, or the largest bra size alphabet you can buy—times three!

I went to meet her in Stone Mountain after she answered my ad on Telepersonals. She said that she was athletic like me, and liked to play sports. She was also a hairdresser and wanted to give me a new hairstyle. Who could pass that up?

While at her house, she told me that she wasn't attracted to me at all and that we could be friends. As I mentioned before, I never could make any friends, so I totally agreed to that. Since she was so blunt to say that she wasn't attracted to me, I let it be known to her that I wasn't attracted to her either. We ordered a couple of large pizzas and she amazed me by styling my hair and eating at the same time!

After she finished my hair, we watched movies and talked. She didn't drink, so having a few beers was out of the question. It was pity because I could've used some to wash down that pizza!

Her phone rang and it just happened to be the stud that she *was* attracted to! They chatted and I continued to watch the movie. I had no problem with it, as we both said we were going to be friends. A few minutes into their conversation, she started crying. The stud was breaking up with her over the phone while I was there! Oh, crap! Bad timing. She got hysterical and threw the phone into the wall smashing it.

I asked if there was anything that I could do, and she told me to bring her something from the upstairs bedroom. I forgot what she asked me to get, but it wasn't a weapon or anything like that! Whatever it was, I couldn't find it, and she came into the room. I was about to leave when she asked me if I would stay the night with her. *Ok?*

Whether we were friends or not, or attracted to each other or not, we slept together that evening. She was hurting and in pain, and I was there to comfort her. That's my story and I'm sticking to it!

The bad news is that she messed up my hair after she fixed it! I'm glad I didn't pay her for it. She eventually patched up things with the stud a few days later and invited me over to meet her. I couldn't come, and I stopped talking to her as well. I found out that I cannot be friends with someone after I've had sex with them. It just seems strange to me. I hope things went well for them.

(There's actually nothing in the briefcase about Debra. I just remember that night and her large breasts!)

"Karen"
(1998)

Karen was the girl that would be dating the ex-girlfriend of Tamela. I think that the ex-girlfriend was cheating on Tamela with Karen, or vise versa, or something like that. Anyway, I met Karen from the chat line and she lived over in Decatur or Ellenwood, somewhere in Dekalb! She was a skinny girl, a former dancer, and she was looking to get into a relationship. Her parents had put her out because she was dating this woman and they were supposed to move in together. Then the woman dumped her! She still couldn't stop talking about her ex-girlfriend even after I came to pick her up!

I had rented a new car to come see her—and she immediately wanted to drive it! Let me drive it! Let me drive it! After showing me her driver's license, I said ok, and asked her where she wanted to go to eat.

Finally, I checked a driver's license from my date before we went out! Surprisingly, she was actually the age she told me she was over the phone!

105

She talked me into letting her drive to a friend's house first! It didn't matter much. This was strictly for entertainment purposes only. I did not like this girl romantically. I actually felt sorry for her, and I knew something wasn't right about her. She thought that she was getting over on me. She wasn't. I just went along for the ride.

She pulled in front of this house with a huge crowd of people in the yard, including Tamela's ex-girlfriend. I recognized her instantly! She was a kind of stocky, possibly Native American, or Puerto Rican stud with long hair tied back in a ponytail.

"Hey, I know that stud!" I said.

Karen said, "Oh, you do. That's my ex-girlfriend! Now, do you see what I am so hurt about losing her?"

Actually, no I didn't. She's cute with good hair, so what? I had it twisted. Karen wasn't trying to use me. Well, not in *that* way, anyway. This girl's self-confidence was shot! Just because her ex-girlfriend was so good-looking, she would let her treat her like a dog just to be with her.

She asked me to stay in the car and I saw what our entire purpose for being there was. The ex-girlfriend, who was sitting with another girl in her lap, would see you in a brand new car, (she wouldn't know it was a rental), with another stud, (she wouldn't know that we weren't together), and would get jealous! She would then get so mad that she would tell that other girl in her lap to leave. Then, she'd point at me to get the hell out of her driveway, and the two of you would go into the house and make mad, steaming hot love! Oh, and you would be back together again and live happily ever after. The end.

Stuff like that never works! The ex-girlfriend wasn't concerned a bit! Karen came stomping back to car crying, turned up the radio, and we drove off. I was worried because she was upset and driving and I was so not trying to go off the road this day! I had gotten over that all that suicidal business from years back and was determined to live now, thank you.

She parked at a restaurant and we went to eat. She spent the whole time blowing up this girl's pager and crying into her food. There wasn't much conversation and to be honest, I was just ready to go home.

I asked her if she wanted me to take her home and she burst into tears. One of the pager messages that she got was her mother telling her not to come back to the house. She had put her out for good. It was true. I actually heard the message for myself. It was something to the likes of:

"Your father and I are disgusted with this gay shit that you are doing! We did not raise you to have sex with women in our house, or to be with women at all! You can not come back here! This is not your home anymore! I don't care want you are doing, or where you sleep tonight! I hope you die of AIDS!"

Therefore, here we were. Now she was homeless. Her mother was crying in the message so I could tell that she still cared about her. She was just tired of the drama. Karen didn't mention to me at first that her parents caught her and the stud in their bed! That wasn't cool at all! No wonder mom is so hot under the collar! I suggested that Karen give her some space.

I then listened as every one of Karen's friends turned her down for a place to crash for a few days. Most of these were mutual friends of her and her ex-girlfriend. They all seemed to be on the ex-girlfriend's side! There was obviously more to the story than Karen had told me. Oh well, I still can't leave someone homeless! I couldn't take her back to my mother's house with me, so I got her a hotel room so we could figure something out the next day. I went home so that she could get some rest.

The next day came and I hadn't figured anything out! I paid for another night at the hotel for her, but another problem was arising. She kept getting sick and vomiting all over the hotel room. She said that she was used to getting sick like this. (I was very glad that I did not sleep with her) I took her to Grady Hospital, and they quickly put her in the Yellow Zone.

I used to work security at Grady, and I knew the sick zones very well and Yellow at the time was for very serious illnesses. I took her pager to find her mother's number to call her. I barely knew this woman and she needed her family and friends—not a stranger.

I told her mother who I was and what had happened to her daughter. I also called several of her friends including the ex-girlfriend and left messages. I waited in the emergency room until her mother arrived and left. I never contacted Karen again, but I did called Grady and they said that she was released two days later. I hope all is well with her.

(The hotel bill from the Days Inn is in the briefcase)

"Mia"
The Lawyer & Her Husband!
(1998)

(I changed names and location this time. "Mia" is an attorney!)

I was just a butch that longed for just one femme to fall in love with and have a family. That was what I wanted! So, why was I getting myself involved in situations where the woman wanted her ex-girlfriend, still lived with her ex-husband, or just wanted to have sex? I don't know really.

Mia wanted sex. Not the same type of sex like London wanted. In fact, I didn't like being with London, because she liked rough sex. I'm not into the biting, the fisting, or the painful stuff! I hate that. I'm the lovemaking, soft kiss, and romantic type. That's what Mia wanted--my soft touch! I was fine with that, but of course, Mia wasn't a person that I could have a relationship. It had to be all about sex. *Why?*

She was an attorney and so was her husband! They were very good attorneys and lived in the Douglasville area. Their house was built from the ground up! It was immaculate!

I would say it was about seven bedrooms, three stories and it was only them and their toddler son who lived there! So, what was this woman doing on a chat line? She was looking for a stud to keep her company while her husband was working late.

I didn't have a car at that time so she would meet me at the gate to Six Flags and take me to her home in her Benz. Mia was an attractive, older woman that loved to entertain me. I like being with her because she was a woman that totally enjoyed me sexually. There wasn't any doubt about that! I was always concerned about being in her home though. It was definitely different from being in the other women's houses on that chat line.

I was in a sunken living room where she had this widescreen television built over the fireplace. I asked to go to the restroom while she was cooking. She pointed it out to me and I walked down this long hallway that lead into this giant foyer with about 20 foot tall cathedral glass ceilings! There was nothing in this room but about three velvet chaise lounges and some plants. You could have put a two-bedroom apartment in that space! They had built a great nest egg for themselves—that's for sure! The bathroom was almost mistaken for a bedroom until I saw a toilet in one corner and a sunken bathtub, like the one that *Scarface* had in the movie, in the center!

I wanted to be with Mia in that tub and she promised me we would! Our *relationship* lasted for only about three weeks, as I was scared out of my wits when her small son walked in on us! She said that he had never done that before, and that he probably thought that I was her husband in the bed with her. I got to thinking that if the son could walk in—then so could her husband one night! Besides, this butch gigolo thing just wasn't for me.

We were drinking some Beringer wine that evening and I took the cork because I knew I wouldn't be back. She kept calling me for days, but I would never answer. That was too much of a risk, and I was getting fond of being with a woman in which I had no future. The tub fantasy would never happen.

(The Beringer wine cork is in the briefcase to remind me of Mia)

I received a promotion from the Telepersonal's and my work shift changed to the late evening hours. I wouldn't get off until around 2AM. The MARTA buses and trains stop service well before then, so for the first couple of weeks I had to walk home to the West End from downtown.

I wasn't bothered the first week, but the second I was cornered on M.L. King Drive by a man that used his car to block my path! I smooth talked him away with a fake promise and address and was relieved. I am not easily punked, but I decided that it would be safer to get an apartment near my job to deter incidents like that one.

My mother didn't want me to get an apartment. She was receiving a lot of money from my paycheck and had just paid off a living room set. She was now renting a new washer and dryer. She was still hooked on that rent-to-own stuff! She had spent over $6,000 in two years on payments for a living room set that was worn after the first six months.

She also didn't want me to take the girls away and had a huge fit that landed her in the emergency room. I assured her that I wouldn't take my daughters, who were now in elementary school, away from her. I was moving just so that I could be closer to the job. She was released a few days later. She had a heart attack over that!

"Kiara"
(1998)

I rented my first apartment alone at 710 Peachtree Street with a great view of the Fox Theatre and the Granada Hotel. I was on the ninth floor and you would think that I had the penthouse how happy I was! The rent was expensive for just a one bedroom but included utilities. I had absolutely no furniture and had to buy one of those blow up air mattresses to sleep on. I refused the rent-to-own deal that my mom's sales representative offered. I wasn't getting caught up in that! It was ok. I had a peace of mind, and it was only about a 15-minute walk down Peachtree to my job. I couldn't wait to bring a woman to my apartment and for us to enjoy the lovely romantic view!

The problem was that it was still 1998, and most of the women I met that year were more into finance than romance! Kiara answered my Telepersonal's ad and I met her and her young son. Now, as far as looks, she put you in the mind of a short Grace Jones. In fact, they could have been twins! She was another former exotic dancer and gave me a show in front of my living room window. She had the lights from the Fox Theatre gleaming in the background to aid her performance!

I took her and her son out to Applebees. I love children, and I am always so patient when they begin to act up, but her son made BeBe's children look like they could host the Bobby Jone's Gospel Hour! Her little man was all in the restaurant kitchen running amok! I chased him down and got him to the seat and promised him some ice cream, (like sweets was what he needed), and he settled down. She told me that I was great with kids and wanted me to meet her friends.

We went somewhere off I-285 to a set of nice apartments near the freeway. I went in and met her friends. They were two gay, Black couples, (two men and two women), that all lived together in this three bedroom. Kiara was the only one that didn't have a mate in her room. This was great for me because I have always wanted to be apart of a gay family-like atmosphere! We listened to music, talked about clubbing, and just had so much fun that evening. Both couples wanted me to come back for Spades card night. I admit that I didn't like Kiara too much, but I would have loved to be apart of a family like that!

Kiara didn't have a job. She had just lost it a few days before we met and wanted me to help find her one. I didn't have any furniture, but rest assured that I still had my computer! It was the only thing in the living room actually! Before she came over one afternoon, I typed her resume, and wrote some jobs I found on a memo pad for her. She told me that she appreciated what I had done, but she was worried about not having $60 to pay her car note that week.

I had just picked up my paycheck from Telepersonals and set aside $100 cash in my billfold for my mother. I had a wallet, but at that time, I always kept my mother's allowance in one of those attaché compartment billfolds. Kiara never asked me for the money, and I never told her that I would give it to her, but I had made up my mind to do so later that evening. I was pouring her son a cup of soda and he spilled it on his pants. She was working on the computer, so I volunteered to change his diaper for her. I told her that I had wrote some jobs on the memo pad in my attaché and asked her to tear the slip out when I left the room.

When we came back, Kiara said that she had to leave because one of her roommates was having a problem. We were supposed to have gone to the movies that afternoon. I walked them to the elevator and asked Kiara to call me to let me know everything was all right. Since my date was cancelled, I decided to take the money to my mother instead. When I got back to my apartment, I opened my billfold and there was only $40 in it now! The slip of paper with jobs was still attached to the memo pad. Kiara had taken $60 out of my billfold while I was changing her son's diaper!

I ran back to the elevator, but by the time I got downstairs and into the parking lot, she was long gone! I was going to *give* her the money, too! I never called her or even confronted her about the money. Heck, what good would it have done? Besides, I'm glad it worked like that because I found out she would steal if she thought she had to. We both knew what she had done and just let it go. Hey, she could have taken the whole $100, so I'll give her a little credit!

I've seen Kiara a few times over the years at clubs, at a Pride event one year, and even one time at Greenbriar Mall with another woman. We will look at each other funny and never say a word to each other. What would we have to say anyway? Whenever I see her, I always laugh and say to myself, "There goes that thief!"

(I tore out the job list and placed in the briefcase)

"Miss Cartier"
(1998)

I found this website and put up a personal ad with my picture on it. I was about 50 pounds lighter back then with some muscles. I thought I looked sexy. I could really meet a good woman off the Internet! I still had a stupid notion that if a woman were on the Internet, then she would probably have a good job, her own place, a car and wouldn't be out for my money or sex. Yep, that was just plain stupid to think!

I saw this femme's ad who said that she liked butch women that, as she put it—reeked with testosterone! That was me. I was hardcore butch so I answered her ad. She seemed quite nice. Miss Cartier had a good job at the tallest building in downtown Atlanta at that time. She was in finances and a computer technician whiz! She did have her own apartment and her car was paid for! If that wasn't enough, she liked cats and had a small son! That was just what I was looking for!

Miss Cartier had an infatuation for cheetah or leopard print or anything like that. I wanted to be debonair and make a lasting impression so I bought her a lamp with a cheetah print shade instead of flowers for our first meeting! It was original and I even got a hug from her. Her son got a train set for his birthday and I volunteer to put it together, of course! I had to show her that I was a handy butch to have around the house!

I got a kiss as I was leaving and we made plans for a formal date that weekend. She even gave me one of her business cards and asked me to meet her for lunch the next day. Well, of course, that tall building wasn't far from where I lived, and I walked down Peachtree to meet her around noon. I waited for her by the lobby elevator.

She never got off the elevator and I called up to her office to ask her if she had forgotten about me. She said that she'd be down in thirty minutes—or she could have said an hour—or three days, whatever! She never did come down however long she said it would take!

I went home and attempted to call and leave her a very nasty voice message. Unfortunately, she picked up the phone before I could!

"I'm sorry about today, but I had a phone call from my ex-girlfriend."

I assumed it was the ex-girlfriend that she said that she wasn't interested in anymore, and that was abusive, and that cheated on her and broke her heart, etcetera—but I didn't bother to ask.

"She said that she is going to buy me a Cartier ring, so I just couldn't resist. Most people don't even know what a Cartier ring is! So, she picked up some points with me, then!"

I had no idea what Cartier was then either, but I dare not tell her that!

"So, you are going to talk this person again just because she is going to buy you a Cartier ring?" (I wondered how much did those rings costs. I found out later. Yep, they were a lot!)

"Yes, of course" she said, "It's Cartier, and obviously you don't know Cartier, do you?"

No, Miss Cartier—I obviously don't. So much for the Internet woman theory!

(The business card she gave me is in the briefcase)

"Myisha"
(1998)

I was beginning to wonder if this year would ever end. I found another lesbian chat line. I will just refer to this one as "MP", since it's still quite popular in the city. I would meet Myisha from this line. She was one of those junk in the trunk sistahs!

Sorry, to be so ghetto, but there was no other way to describe this femme's backside! I'm not even one for that in a woman, remember, but she was extremely nice in that department. She met me at my job and I gave her some money to be me an outfit for the club that evening. It was a bad idea!

No, she didn't run off with it like Kiara probably would have! She bought me an imitation FUBU shirt! It was PUBU or something like that! Whatever it was, I shouldn't have worn it that night! We rode the bus that evening with a bunch of high school students that had just left a football game and I was roasted! Those kids almost had me crying! Myisha thought the crap was so funny!

We went to the EconoLodge to spend the evening because I still didn't have a bed at my apartment. We bought some drinks, settled into the room until that morning, and put the "Do Not Disturb" sign on the door. We were in full lesbian contact when one of the housekeepers opened the door with some towels. Myisha jumped out of the bed and ran naked to the door grabbing the towels from the woman who was just mumbling something in Spanish! It was hilarious and I know she was embarrassed, but we did have the sign on the door!

Myisha reminded me a lot of Nichelle. She wanted to go out, have fun with me, and just stay free. She never misled me. I just wanted more than she wanted to give. She further squashed that theory Rose gave me about woman opening their bed to you always wanting more. I guess that only applied to femme virgins, because I never met another femme that had that same outlook!

I just stopped contacting her because I wanted so much more than good sex. I've seen her several times over the years as well and we always speak, but that's all.

(The hotel key is in the briefcase to remind me of Myisha)

Chapter 12

1999 Was No Party

My mother would go into the hospital more and more during the first part of 1999. She had developed what I thought was Alzheimer's disease. She couldn't remember many things she did throughout the day and it was becoming much more difficult for her to take care of herself and the girls. I couldn't afford the rent at 710 Peachtree anymore because Telepersonals was closing their U.S. offices and moving operations to Canada. Some of us employees were offered jobs if we relocated. I wanted to go very badly and take my daughters out of the United States, but my mother needed me here.

Mom would get angry and would accuse me of trying to take the girls away from her. She started to call the office and talking to my co-workers. She would leave messages that she loved me and that she was doing fine at home. My co-workers at Telepersonals were good people, and for the most part, would treat her as if she was their mother when she called. It got to the point where they would know that if I wasn't at work, it was because I was home with my mother and daughters.

I didn't answer any personal ads during most of 1999. Mom and the girls had the majority of my attention and I didn't even bother to check my ad for responses. During midyear, my mother starting listening to and watching only gospel. She used to watch many different movies with me and the girls, but now it was only gospel. I took it as a sign that she was preparing herself for transition.

She got a visit from two Jehovah Witness members one day and started inviting them in for fellowship. She really wanted people to talk to, and she hadn't been to a church service in years because of her illness. I came over after work to give her some money for my daughter's school, and the women were in our living room.

I usually wear my slacks and a dress shirt, and am obvious to anyone. When I entered the apartment, I spoke to the women who gave a judging look and only nodded back. One of them asked my mother if I was her daughter. *OK? You would think that a twenty-nine year old woman could speak for herself if you'd ask her!*

My mother answered yes, and then the women began to ask me of my religious beliefs.

"So, where is your church home? Do you believe in the commandments? Do you attend any Sunday services?"

I wanted to explain how I worshipped God within myself and not at a building. I wanted to say that I don't give money to the collection plate at a church and prefer to do random acts of charity to people on the street that I don't know. I wanted to say how I knew the greatest commandment is "love", and that I believed that God loves me as much as He does everyone else and is pleased as long as I pass the love He gives me to all of His children that cross my path.

Nevertheless, I just told them, "No. Yes, I believe love is the greatest commandment, and no, I don't go to church because I have to go to work on Sunday."

The older one had to make sure that I knew that there were more commandments than to love people. She especially wanted to stress the "Honor Thy Father and Mother" commandment.

"You know that a child that doesn't honor his or her mother isn't pleasing in the eye of Jehovah? Have you done right by your mother?"

Of course I had! But, it was none of her business! I didn't answer. I'm always courteous to people, but you can tell when I get upset with someone. It's never ok to come into one's home and judge them based solely upon their sexual orientation, or because their religious beliefs are different from yours.

Bernard just happened to walk in at that moment, as we were going shopping for Tee's birthday gift. He was about to make a turn for the door after he saw the women! Too late.

"So, is this your husband? How are you, sir? It's good to see that you are sticking by this woman! Do you have a church home?"

He answered them and quickly made a motion for us to leave. He had heard what the woman asked me about my mother and didn't care for it at all. Bernard knew how much I took care of my mother and had seen it for years now.

My mother and I used to take our religion and faith quite seriously. We were members of Dr. Barbara King's Hillside Chapel on Cascade, and joined even before she built the Church in the Round. My mother and I didn't buy those $20 bricks when they built Centennial Olympic Park, but we were first in line to buy one of Dr. Kings' $10 bricks to help build the new church. We went there until problems with my mother's oxygen tank and parking made it a chore to make it to either service.

That was the last church that we belonged to after Father Abraham had passed away. All the churches where we were ever members believed in the loving everyone regardless of who they were. Now, that she was ailing and couldn't get around, she was just listening to whoever would come to her door. I had wished it was the Mormons that knocked!

All of this time, my mother sat quietly as they tried to convince Bernard and her that his Baptist, and her Truth Center church beliefs were not acceptable in God's sight.

"I bet your church accepts the homosexual! They aren't welcome at the Kingdom Hall!"

My mother quickly yelled, "No, we don't! Well, I don't accept them!"

I left my mother the money on the table and stormed out of her apartment with Bernard tagging behind me. I could hear my daughter's crying to go with us, and I asked Bernard to go get and get them. My mother was crying now telling us to not come back, and I could see the Jehovah Witness women were hugging her as we drove off.

"That was not my mother, Bernard! She's sick. That medicine is making her act that way. My mother would have never turned on me like that, or brought those judging people into our home!"

After I had lost the apartment in Midtown, I rented an office on Mitchell Street where I had started a business doing income tax returns and teaching computer classes. I had to do something because the Telepersonals job would end later this year. That same day, after we picked up Tee's birthday gift, I asked Bernard to drop us off at my office. I still had my blow up mattress and an empty area in the office for the girls to sleep. My mother called Bernard and left a message that I could stay with at that office or with him. She didn't want me to come back to her house. I could tell that those women were still there with her.

I moved to first shift on the job so that the girls were in school when I worked. Even though my mother lived across the street from the school, I had to catch the bus and take them all the way to M. Agnes Jones from East Point. It was only a few weeks, because my mother called crying and apologized for her behavior. She wanted me to bring the girls back to her house to stay. I did, because they were missing her. I did not return to her house, but lived in my office on Mitchell Street to keep the peace.

In another attempt at a college degree, I enrolled at Georgia Perimeter College. I received unemployment after leaving Telepersonals, and had enough money to pay for at least one class. I chose English Literature and was excited about being in a college class again, even if I was twenty-nine years old now!

I was in the top five of my English class, and was surprisingly one of the youngest students. Our instructor was an author of many books, and she would be the first to point out that I should write to relieve stress. I began writing screenplays and several fiction novels, which I could not tell you where I have those now if you offered to buy them from me! I kept the briefcase, but didn't have a specific place for my writings, and some of them may have ended up in file thirteen.

My entire college career has consisted of Georgia State University, Clayton State University, Atlanta Metropolitan College and Georgia Perimeter, I have managed enough credits for an associate degree in pre-pharmacy—which I have never applied for. I always had to leave college for some reason, but mostly to take care of mother and my daughters. This time was no exception. I left after just two classes and another restroom incident.

I always have a hard time when it comes to using public restrooms. I can count numerous times when security has followed me into the women's restroom because they thought I was a man. I usually don't even use the public restroom unless my girlfriend insists I come in there with her. It's just one of those things I have to live with.

After I sold my used books back to the college store, I went into the women's campus restroom. There just happened to be one of the women's softball team players in there at the sink. She was wearing her full uniform. I had on my usual men's dress shirt and slacks.

A young, Asian woman came into the restroom and saw us both. She almost screamed for days!

"Isn't this the women's restroom! What are you doing in here? Or, I'm *I* in the wrong place? Oh, my goodness!"

The softball player didn't even bother to answer her, but just laughed. Just as I was about to clear things up, some other women walked in, and she decided to ask them instead.

"Is this the women's restroom, or the men's restroom?"

I was beginning to feel sorry for the young, Asian woman until she laughed after asking that! She knew that both of us were women, she was just making a *funny*, or rather trying to make one. Her new audience just thought she was being stupid and paid her no attention at all. She then had the nerve to bring the joke back to me—one of the butts of it!

"So, is this the women's room, or the men's room?"

I looked over to my softball friend, who just shook her head. It was on me to come up with a clever comeback.

"Well, you are in here now, so what difference does it make? Pop a squat or stand—it's your choice!"

I got a thumbs up and even a laugh from one of the other women! The woman murmured something to me in Korean and went into a stall. I've forgotten the word now, but to this day I wondered if it was a Far East homosexual slur.

"Marie"
(1999)

Dating someone was the last thing on my mind. My mother was still very ill. She went back to the doctor and they changed her medication again. She was also still on 24-hour oxygen and had tanks delivered to the house. Medicaid had paid for her a home monitoring system and even a hospital bed. Her apartment was beginning to look more and more like a hospital ward.

She went outside in nothing but her gown one chilly morning and our neighbor had to help her back inside. Tim and I would take turns making sure that she was all right throughout the day. It was a rough time.

While in the Telepersonals computer room, I noticed that there was a response in my box. It was a woman named Marie from Brooklyn. She had two teenage children and owned a house in Cobb County. We met at Dave and Busters and hit it off just fine. She was a little older than I was, so I thought that would be what I needed. I told her about what my mother was going through, and she wanted to help with her as much as she could.

I remember going over to Marie's house and planning a barbecue for her after work. I went to Wal-Mart and bought a new grill! I was finally in my element! I cooked hamburgers, chicken, and steaks in her backyard. She even let me set a table, and for the first time in over twenty years, I had a family style dinner. She loved animals and had two playful large dogs. I actually felt like I could have a future with this woman. Marie was more than willing to try it.

However, Marie was in no condition to promise a future with anyone. I didn't know it at the time, but she would be the first in a string of women that I would meet over the next 5 years that had been abused by men. Up until now, it was just sex, gold diggers, husbands and ex-husbands—now it will be combinations of these because of heterosexual relationship abuse! I was about to get a first helping of it at the end of the century.

Marie had been divorced from her husband for some time, but she was still using his last name. I would see packages that he would send her for his kids and he would have her maiden name on them instead of his. During the time that I dated her, she found out that he had remarried—without telling her. This totally angered her and her daughter! I heard a big argument that she had over the phone with him because of that and the fact that he was on his way to Atlanta to spend time with the daughter and introduce her to the new wife!

Marie had turned to the gay life like most woman abused by men. She wasn't really gay. She was looking for an escape from heterosexuality and abuse, as do most battered women. That is not the answer for them, and they should seek guidance from a counselor or an organization, because in the end it will only hurt them—and the women that they date while seeking solitude!

There was a pool bar near Piedmont Park called Duprees and that is where Marie and I used to shoot pool. I was with her that evening when her ex-husband was in town visiting their daughter. She had dropped her off at the hotel near the airport.

Marie was really drinking that night and it was clear that the situation was bothering her, as she would yell at me all evening about any and every little thing. I couldn't do anything right by her that night!

When it rains, it does pour! I got a call that evening from Tim's girlfriend. My mother had been rushed to the hospital. She had a stroke. My daughters were at their other sitters, Bernard was on the road, and I was stuck in Midtown with my car in Cobb County.

Tim didn't know if he should have them put my mother on the life support machine. He was much older than I was! Why did I have to make that decision?

I said, "Yes, please tell them to put her on the machine!" His girlfriend was more interested in when I would get to the hospital and kept asking me where I was!

For years, I had always been the one to go to the hospital with my mother. I would be the one to stay there to make sure everything was proper. One time I even caught them giving her someone else's medicine in her IV and immediately called her doctor! Yes, I agree that I had been the one there for mother for years, but I still wasn't her only child! I was the youngest, the only girl and apparently the only one capable of making important decisions on her health. Why put all of that on me?

I told Marie about what was happening with my mother and she got an emergency phone call. Things were not going well for her daughter and her father at the hotel either! Marie said that we would get her daughter, take me to my car, and I could drive to the hospital to see my mother.

When we got to the hotel, Marie asked me to wait downstairs while she went up. I got another call from Tim's girlfriend. I told her what was happening, and that I was on the way to my car, so that I could get to the hospital. I admit that now I was totally pissed off at how my brother's girlfriend was implying that I didn't care about my mother!

I had always been there for her! I dropped out of college because she was sick! I worked overtime so that I could pay for her rental stuff! You could say that I even *gave* her my daughters so that she wouldn't be lonely! I had spent my whole life making sacrifices for my mother! All I had ever asked for in return was to have a partner and a family! Did I have that? No! I just keep meeting women with problems, and problems, and bullshit—and *more* problems!

Speaking of which, at that moment Marie got off the elevator with her daughter. They were both crying, and in a tight embrace, went rushing right past me through the hotel door. Did they see me? If I had been a second earlier in step, then I would have been left! They got into the car, started it, and backed up! I had to tap on the roof of the car to stop them.

Hello? I know your ex-husband is married to someone else now, and that sucks, but you guys are forgetting someone!

Marie had forgotten that I was even there! When I got into the car I didn't hear a "Sorry, we were about to leave you", or anything to that nature. They didn't even speak to me. I just heard them talk to each other the whole ride of how the father was a jackass, and how he would "pay later", and how the new wife was ugly and wore glasses, and so much more that I was very glad when we pulled into her driveway!

They got out and rushed into the house still without saying a word to me. I could hear Marie now giving her son the full details about the ghastly visit from their father.

Ok. Well, I'll just be leaving now to check on my mother. Later, ok? Bye.

I got into the car and rushed to Crawford Long Hospital. My mother was on the top floor and hooked up numerous machines. I cringed as I noticed an incision on her neck where they'd cut for her to breathe. I thought how we had argued earlier that week while those Jehovah Witness women were in the house, and how she had told me that she didn't want me to come home.

I asked God not to let her leave me like this. Not on night where I wasn't there, or couldn't be here. Not when I didn't even know what she said or what she did before. Not now, God. Please, don't take her now. Let her live the see the Glory, like I've always asked of You.

Marie called the next day to see how my mother was and to apologize. My mother fully recovered and was sent home some days later.

Marie had never really talked to her kids about being a lesbian. After the incident with her ex-husband, then it was clear that her children really needed mother. I called and they would be playing Scrabble or another game and she wouldn't answer. They would tell her that she was spending too much time with this woman and would wonder why she would call so much.

She mentioned that she attempted to tell her son one time, and he almost started to cry. I would recall her saying that he would want to even hurt his father if he had turned her into a lesbian. She didn't know how to explain why I would spend the night in her bed and be there in the morning when they would go to school. She said that she just couldn't tell them, and it made a lot of sense.

Chapter 13

The Garden of Glory

They always say be careful what you pray for, because sometimes you'll get it. Sometimes specifics can get screwed!

For example, I saw this *Tales from the Crypt* one time where a woman prayed to marry a man that would inherit a lot of money. She ended up marrying a man and *won* a million dollars! After she told the man she was leaving him, he killed her—thus inheriting her million dollars! Sometimes things are twisted!

Where was I New Years eve in 1999? Did I have a fall out shelter or some flashlights ready for Y2K? Nope! I had another apartment in East Atlanta and was on my balcony launching fireworks into the sky! My mother called and said that she didn't think that she'd make it to see the year 2000, but she did! I must have drunk about two full bottles of Sutter Home by myself!

I called Marie to say Happy New Year! By then, she was still upset about her ex-husband and didn't really care about anything. When I called, she was doing her daughter's hair and wasn't excited about the New Year, or century, at all!

I had left a computer over to her house and she had asked me to come get it. She had made her decision not to tell her kids about us and wanted me to remove anything I had from her house. I guess she was still mourning the fact that her husband had moved on without her. I picked up my computer a few months later on the way to the Farmers Market.

My mother and I aren't Jewish, but we celebrated Passover. It was a tradition started back from Father Abraham's church back in the seventies. After he died and the church terminated, some of his members kept the tradition. We would go into the book of Exodus and read how we were supposed to get the lamb on a certain day and eat it.

Each year, I would buy the lamb and my mother and I would have the feast. In 2000, I bought the lamb and we were about to have Passover, and something occurred to me just as I was reading the scripture. It was March. We were supposed to do Passover in April! It's always in April! I looked at my mother and she had a blank look on her face that I will never forget.

"Mom, why are doing this a month early? Why didn't we notice?"

She didn't respond. I laughed about it, but she didn't.

"Gail"
(2000 – 2004)

In March 2000, I tried club promotions, and started a gay Monday night at a club called Taste on Peachtree Street. It bummed out after just four weeks! It was around the same time that the old Marquette building was closing and I had recruited some of the staff to help me out on Monday nights. It wasn't enough! People just wouldn't come.

On one of my nights, there was a group of three women that showed up at the club. The short one that wore a red dress would be bold enough to give her number to my door person to pass on to me. I thought at first that she wanted to perform at the club. I called her days later and she said that she was interested in dating me. Well, this was a change of pace. No woman had ever come up to me in a club before. Gail would be the first woman that I would ever talk to that I didn't meet off a chat line or personals ad.

After a typical, quick lesbian courtship, Gail moved in with me in my new East Atlanta apartment. I had introduced her to my mother and I would sometimes stay the night with mom, while she would keep my daughters in East Atlanta. One night, while I was watching television with mom, she asked me to call an ambulance for her. I knew that she was sick because she would never *ask* to go to the hospital. The medics came, but I couldn't go because I had no baby sitter for the children and Gail was still at work. As I saw the ambulance go down our driveway, I saw her in the back window looking back into the apartment.

Mom was back at Crawford Long on that same machine. She would be on it for days and couldn't talk. I visited her and took the girls to see her whenever they would let me. Gail and I alternated being at my mom's house and our apartment so that the girls could sleep in their beds. I would also learn that Gail was adopted, and didn't know where her biological family lived. After all these years, her mother had just given her the name of her biological father and she wanted to find out where he was. I said that I would help if I could.

I was making dinner for the Gail and the girls when the phone rang. I answered and no one said anything, they were just pressing buttons. I thought for a minute and then I knew it was my mother! She was still on the machine and couldn't talk, but had sneaked and got the phone to call me! We had a conversation with her pressing buttons either once or twice to respond! When I told her goodbye, then she pressed the button for a long time! That was my mother!

The next time she called was that morning and she could talk! I didn't make it to the phone in time and she left a message on my machine to call her back. I did and I told her that I was shocked to hear her voice! She asked why and I really couldn't tell her. I just didn't know.

"They are about to put me in my room and I'll be back home in a few days. I just have to go and get an X-ray and I'll be in my room," she said.

I was going to wake up the girls to talk to her, but she said let them sleep and she will talk to them when she got into her room. I told her that I loved her.

"I love you too. Talk to you later. Bye."

I started making breakfast for the girls. About an hour later, Tim called me crying. He said that Crawford Long had called and that mom had taken a turn for the worst. I told him that was ridiculous because I had just spoken to mom a few moments ago. He told me that I needed to get down to the hospital fast.

When I arrived at the hospital every top physician at Emory University and Crawford Long Hospital administrator that was on staff that day greeted me and offered condolences.

"Are you the lady that she spoke to on the phone before she went into X-ray?"

I said that I had just talked to her and she told me that she was going into X-ray before she was taken into her room.

The doctors and administrators of Crawford Long Hospital expressed their "deepest apology" as my mother, who had been on 24-hour oxygen for the past 7 years of her life was left unattended, without oxygen, lying flat down in the X-ray waiting area on a gurney by an orderly for over 10 minutes. My mother barely slept in her bed for years because she complained of not being able to breathe in a prone position.

To this day, I still can't sleep lying on my back because I can still imagine my mother gasping for air and no one coming to help her.

I would go into the room and see her. She was in a coma and although she was moving from time to time, the doctors would say those were miniature seizures. They had called my brothers and me up there to tell us that we should start making funeral arrangements.

I brought the girls to see her on her birthday, April 28, 2000, and they would tell me later, that even though the doctor's would say that it was impossible, that she spoke to them and told them that she loved him. I would get her last phone call and her last words and I would know why we made the mistake to celebrate the Passover a month too early. It was because during the real Passover, she would be in a coma.

God wanted us to do it one last time together.

(I was going to type more, but I'll end it there)

She would remain in a coma from April 6, 2000 to May 10, 2000 when she would pass away. I thought about how over 250 visitors came to see her during her mastectomy in the seventies, and how the room was full of flowers. Now, it would just be some flowers from me and a card from a friend in her room when we would clear it away. She was laid to rest the day before Mother's Day in 2000.

We didn't sue Crawford Long Hospital only because my eldest brother, Perry, was against it. The attorney, Tim and I had felt that it wouldn't have looked right if the eldest son protested.

Remember, when I mentioned be careful what you pray for because sometimes specifics get twisted?

For over 20 years when my mother was sick, I would always prayed to God to let my mother live to see the Glory.

I had heard her say it from time to time that is what she wanted to live to see, so I started praying for it, too!

I always prayed that prayer and He did what just I asked him.

(In Loving Memory of My Mother)

Mary Hellen Willingham Goodson

April 28, 1933 to May 10, 2000

Laid to rest in the "Garden of Glory"
at Kennedy Memorial Gardens
Ellenwood, Georgia

December 24, 2006
(2:22 AM)
Lithonia Georgia USA
(Location: My Writing & *Drinking* Closet)

It's Christmas Eve 2006 and I'm in my closet by the computer with a bottle of Peach Vodka. Merry Christmas to all! I took a couple of days off from writing to finish my Christmas shopping. I bought Vee that Guitar Hero II video game and got Tee a digital camera so that she will stop asking to use mine. I bought Bernard one of those massaging back heated covers. It's safe to write those gifts in this book because none of them are going to log on to this computer and read it before the morning anyway! Ha..ha!

By now, you've realized that although I'm clever with technology, business, and all of that whohaa—I'm really bad at relationships and friends! I was dealt a bad hand in my opinion. I got all the geek cards, you know! I was given the smarts and stuff, but not the mojo that gets you the house full of friends every weekend and the great steady girlfriend! Some heterosexual men and other butches know what I mean, well at least the geeky ones do anyway!

(Bear in mind that I am drinking alcohol as I write. Alcohol is a depressant, and in my case, it's truth serum! Which is why I never drink around people I have secrets from—or ex-girlfriends, or law enforcement, or, well—you get the point!)

A dude named Ashton has this reality television show called *Beauty and the Geek,* for those highly intelligent guys that can't get a good-looking babe! Growing up they all wished that they could do like those boys did in that movie, *Weird Science*, and *make* them a girlfriend! Well, Ashton felt their pain and made them a reality show! I wished he would do one for the geeky women and the geeky lesbians like me! I watch that show and just stay, "Damn, you know those two would have NEVER hooked up!"

Don't get me wrong, I think I'm quite attractive and look great in a two-piece suit! I've spent years looking for my *beauty*.

I've never had much faith in finding her, because I found out how most of this lesbian stuff works. Heterosexuals don't realize it, or understand it, and neither do must of our gay male colleagues—it's hard for butch and dominant lesbians to find that "athletic" looking partner.

I used the term *athletic* to not appear shallow, because I just don't know what other term to use! People are going to say that I am shallow anyway no matter what word I use, so I'm just going to flow with that one. Just like being butch, or "feminine" as it refers to a gay male, is a stereotypical way of "looking gay" to heterosexual people, there is another myth out there that **ALL** lesbians are unattractive, overweight women.

(Let me clarify that I am not implying that they go hand in hand—I've seen some very beautiful, overweight women in my lifetime! Likewise, I've also seen some unattractive, thinner women!)

That is why some talk shows have those, "Do I look gay?" shows and people are like "No way that she's gay, etc!" People, especially heterosexuals, don't expect extremely beautiful, in-shape women to be lesbian. They mostly dismiss them as bisexual or "needing a good man"! Some butches, including myself, have had that same theory for years. (See *JohnTre's Guide to Sexual Orientation & Acceptance in the U.S.*)

The majority of lesbians that *are* attracted to butch or aggressive women I have found to be larger women. Lesbians don't want to admit this, and people are going to get upset by reading this, too—but let the truth be told! If butches see a femme that is thin, or girly-girly, we automatically *assume* that she is a lipstick lesbian or into other femmes. Those select few femmes that are into butches wonder why no butches will come up to them and say hello. That's why! Most of us assume that you are not interested.

I guess that is why I've always taken any woman has come into my life. Looks, height, weight or whatever has never mattered to me, because I just wanted to be with someone. That's probably been the case on their end as well, as I don't think the majority of women that I've spent time with were even attracted to me. They just wanted to see what they could get out of me.

I think that's the problem with most of us! Heterosexual or homosexual, we date people that we don't want to just not to be alone! That is one of the reasons that we cannot be faithful, and that we end up being used and disappointed. I had to learn a valuable lesson in life, and that's why I'm in my bedroom closet, drinking vodka alone on Christmas Eve! I would have saved myself a lot of heartache and pain if I'd just not settled for any woman that answered my ad or came along.

But, enough of all that! I still have to take you through my four-year domestic partnership with Gail. That's going to call for another drink of vodka.

However, you know I like to give you these present day updates. How am I? Well, that depends on how you feel about someone writing a book in a closet at 3:00 AM with hard liquor on Christmas Eve! I still have not plugged my phone back or have checked my emails. I am still shut off from civilization. I am still thinking about that last woman, who you will come to know as "Jess" in the last chapters of this book. I'm guessing she and everyone else is enjoying the holiday season, and I am putting on a good show for my girls to make them think that I'm enjoying it too! Humbug.

Just to reassure you, I have no suicidal tendencies whatsoever! I'm just flat out depressed, in pain and drinking—*but writing*—and hey again, that's a good thing! I'm headed into the kitchen for a refill and then I'll continue. I have to remember to fill up the ice trays next time. Cheers!

--L.A. JohnTre

Chapter 14

Unhappily Married,
(The sequel: "JohnTre and The Wannabe")

My mother was the focus of my life. Now, at the beginning of the new millennium, everything would change. I was now going to be a full time parent to my daughters. Even more, I had met Gail, who would be the last woman that I would ever date to meet my mother. I thought for sure that was a sign that this was the woman that I was supposed to be with forever!

I called Marie the day after my mother passed away and left a message. She never returned it or called me ever again, and changed her number some months later. Amazing how people can act like they care and they just don't! She had met my mother and had talked to her several times. I thought she could have at least expressed her condolences. Anyway, I mistook Marie for my *Joan*. She had some of her qualities, but eh, whatever!

Joan who, you ask? Well, one of my ideal wife characters would have to be *Joan*, from the television show, *Girlfriends*. Joan is the lawyer character played by Diana Ross's daughter. She has a great career, she craves romance and is very diverse with her cooking, the way she decorates her house and her overall style is just perfect for me. No wonder her character can't find a good man on the show. She's a perfect lesbian housewife! (Note to self: contact the show writers about that!)

Gail was far from *being Joan*. In fact, she was more of a combination of the other three *Girlfriends'* characters and even some of the male character, *William*. That's actually not an insult considering what happened later. I knew that Gail wasn't the one for me, as I knew of the others, but we were both going through some rough times and needed someone to be there. My mother was still in a coma the first of our relationship, so having her and her friends around the house helped a great deal. After mom passed away, I had to plan a completely new path for my life that included raising both of my daughters. I would have Bernard's financial support for Tee, but only government and work support for Vee, as you remember, William was nowhere to be found!

I needed a wifely figure now. In the lesbian world, we call them *wifeys*. Let's face it! I have always been both of my daughter's best friend when it came down to computers and video games and watching cartoons, but I when it comes to motherly stuff, I am totally lost! I can't comb their hair or even think about going to the girl stores and pick out clothing.

My favorite part of the movie, *Poetic Justice*, was when Janet Jackson combed Tupac Shakur's little girl's hair at the end. That was so sweet! He was helpless about doing his daughter's hair as most father's are! I told you that butches are as close to heterosexual men that you can find. We are men, that aren't really men.

Now, you have some men that *can* do their daughter's hair and you have some butches that can do hair as well. It isn't the norm for the man to learn. He did because obviously he wanted to. However, it's no big deal if the butch learns because she is *still* a woman? That sucks!

When I first started dating Gail she would do both of my daughter's hair. Later on, she would say that I should learn how to do my daughter's hair myself. I responded that I didn't want to do it, and that I wasn't cut out to do it!

"Say you asked your father to do your hair? If he said that he didn't know how, and he was a single parent, would you also tell him that he needed to *learn* how to do it because he had a daughter?"

"No", Gail would say. "You are their mother! Butch or not, then you should still know how to do your own daughter's hair! You are still not their father."

(She just did not understand!)

Gail was at work and I was over to my mother's house cleaning out the apartment. The rental sales representative that had known my mother for years came to pick up the furniture that she had put thousands of dollars into and still didn't own. Someone had already broken into the home and stolen the appliances from the kitchen while mom was in the hospital, so he just got the living room and bedroom set. That was a burden lifted. I would miss my mother dearly, but not paying all those rental store bills!

Those Jehovah Witness women came by that day as well to see my mother. I was always very cordial to them.

"Hello. Sorry, but Mrs. Goodson is in the hospital in a coma. She is passing away. I can give you her room number at hospital."

They both said something about not having time to go to the hospital and that even if they did, they had other members that do the missionary work. They were just the ones that come out to fellowship. Actually, I didn't know that.

They left me a few *Watchtowers* and went about their way. There was no need to ask if they could come in and fellowship. Aside from the fact that I was the condemned homosexual, I was also busy cleaning.

A woman from Conyers called and wanted to talk to Gail. She had some information about her birth father. Gail had called several people in the phone book that had the last name that was given to her by her adopted mother. She asked them if they had a little girl that was taken away from them almost 25 years ago. She lucked up and called her father's sister-in-law! Even better news was that her father lived in Atlanta, just a few miles away.

Gail got the news when she returned from work and we called the sister-in-law for her father's address. I knew instantly where he lived and took Gail to see him. I was extremely excited for her to finally see him after all those years and to share in that moment. I hadn't seen my bank robber father, Nathaniel, since I was 12 years old. I would do some Internet searching to find out that he was incarcerated in Dekalb for rape for two years. Although the law says that he has to register where he lives with the state, I was still unable to locate him. I had just wanted him to meet his granddaughters. *Oh, well.*

During that Easter of 2000, while my mother was still in the coma, I would drive Gail and her friends to Conyers to meet the rest of her family. It was a big one! She had sisters, brothers, nieces, nephews, aunts, uncles and cousins galore! A happy time for her and an ironic, painful time for me, as I would be with someone that had found something that I was always searching for.

She had found her biological family and I had taken her to meet them, while my mother, the final glue to the piece of the family I had, was in the hospital dying. It was one of the tasks that would have a toll on me. However, I wasn't jealous of Gail. I was happy because I had hoped that I could possibly be apart of her family too.

That would be a problem because Gail wasn't ready to come out to her new bio family. I understood that, but her friends that were living with us at the time thought that she should let everyone know whom I was. I attended my mother's funeral alone, because Gail went to Conyers to be with her new family. When she came back, both her friends and I noticed that Gail was behaving differently after being around them.

There was nothing much to say to that. I could blame staying with Gail on the fact that I was depressed about losing my mother, but I won't. She gave me so many signs that she wasn't ready for a relationship with anyone. I just didn't need to be alone.

Gail was abused by a boyfriend for years and escaped him to come to Atlanta. I didn't know that I would be her first lesbian relationship. That is never a good thing for a butch like me! She had a young daughter that lived with her adopted mother. Throughout the time that we were first together, she would tell me that one day she would like her daughter to be back with her. I thought that it would be wonderful to raise three girls together, so I vowed to help her with that.

We moved to the Fair Street bottom area so that the girls could continue in school. Gail would frequent the Marquette Club, and although she would even have several men approach her, she would be amazed that people would take her for a butch! When I met Gail, she had on a dress, and she had some femme tendencies, but she was never truly a femme. I didn't notice it, or want to notice it, but I remember someone asking me who had the *upper hand* in our relationship? I would say that it was me, of course. People would think otherwise, or would think that we were in a butch-butch relationship. That was SO not the case! At least I didn't think so!

(For the record, just because a butch may say that she has the upper hand in a relationship, does not imply that she is trying to boss the relationship or demean her partner. I used the exact words of the person asking the question, but she simply meant who was the "butch" and who was the "femme" in our relationship)

Gail gave me a "way out" just before my thirtieth birthday. She said that she was finding men more attractive again and wanted me to give her space. I am so bad at those! I recognize "way outs" all of the time and usually just try to ignore them! Gail was clearly saying that she didn't want to be with me and wanted us to be friends. Several things were wrong with that for me.

One, I cannot be friends with people that I've been intimate with! That is public knowledge to those that know of me. Two, I had just lost my mother three months prior, had no family or friends that understood who I was, and she was the last woman that would ever meet my mother! I pressured Gail to stay with me and she did. So, now you can take what she did for the next four years and say that I brought it on myself if you'd like, because I didn't take the "way out" she gave me years before.

We moved around a lot. We couldn't keep jobs very long, and I found myself trying to promote my web design business and computer training. One year we settled into an apartment on Ashby Street just down the street from the new Marquette Building. It was perfect for Gail, who still enjoyed going to the club. I had slowed down my clubbing.

I was sinking more into trying to be a parent. I wanted a family orientated life, and when your mate doesn't want that as well—then there will be problems! Gail and I would argue about her clubbing and her uncanny way of meeting people and allowing them into the house. We had to move away from the first apartment we had, when her other friends started a ruckus with one of my neighbors.

I don't allow many people into my house and Gail had the ability to have people flock to her. All of these people weren't necessarily good people, and you don't want to bring everyone into your home around your children. I was highly protective of my daughters when they were that young of age and Gail didn't care for that. After all, this was my first time raising them without my mother's intervention.

After a huge argument one night, Gail went to the Marquette. A few days later, we saw this dude in the grocery store that Gail was trying to avoid. She said that she knew him at one time and that he was always trying to get her to come home with him. She eventually spoke to him and even introduced us.

Gail started to get sick after that weekend. I would take her fishing to get her some fresh air, as I thought it was the house that was making us sick. The roof plaster fell one evening, almost hitting the girls in the head as they slept. They were living over to Bernard's house while the landlord fixed the ceiling. Gail and I both had headaches after the roof incident, so we thought that was the cause of it.

I would get better but Gail would still be sick after a few months. Finally, we took her to Crawford Long for an exam. She was in the emergency room all day, and I had to pick up the girls from school and take them to East Point.

I remember us joking in the waiting room about how it would be funny if she were sick because she was pregnant. Yeah, funny! We had been together almost two years! I was driving back to the hospital when she called and told me that our *joke* – was no joke! She was indeed pregnant. Three months pregnant! I asked her how that could be and who was the father? It wasn't me! That we knew for sure!

"Do you remember that guy that came up to us in the grocery store?" she started.

Well, that explains why she was avoiding him, doesn't it?

We had researched trying to have a baby by artificial insemination. She said that she wanted another child, and I did too, so we even looked at possible donors over the Internet. The costs were beyond our budget so I agreed that we would look into Gail getting pregnant the old-fashioned way. There was talk of C. Anthony as a donor for us and another person that she knew. I would have agreed to that! However, I would have never agreed to the person in the grocery store! It was cheating and her only reason for it was that she was angry with me that evening.

For a second opinion, I asked our neighbor, GiGi Labelle. She was a drag performer at the old Marquette and kind of a mentor for the lesbian couple that lived next door! She had positive look on the matter as I had expected.

"You were going to pay for the sperm anyway! At least you saved some money and you never know. This can be the blessing that brings you two closer."

We would go to a local Emory lesbian doctor for her OB-GYN care. I would find out that Gail was carrying a boy! Just what we both wanted! We had already picked out the name for him almost a year earlier and both agreed. I did become quite happy about the pregnancy and it didn't matter where the sperm had come from just as GiGi said! Gail had made a promise to me to not even involve the guy in our son's life. If he asked later down the line about his father, then we agreed to tell him everything.

That promise was broken just as Gail began to show. She happened to be at Five Points one day when the guy walked up and noticed that she was pregnant. She said that she told him without him asking and he quickly denied it! *(Well, yeah?)*

"I thought you said that you weren't going to tell him, Gail?" I was really upset. It doesn't make any since to me for people to make promises that they are going to keep!

"I just saw him and thought he should know. We may be able to get assistance from him to take care of the baby. He can buy diapers and help, too. I'm not trying to get stuck with taking care of a child without the father's help."

You can imagine the argument that followed that! Not only was she implying that I wouldn't be there to take care of her and the baby as I promised, but it was a small slap in the face for not having William around to take care of Vee. If you have a real butch then they will take care of the baby just like a good biological father. Strong butch-femme lesbian parenting couples know that our relationships work closely similar to those of the heterosexual nature. The butch takes on the fathering role and can be a great one if she is a real butch!

As for William, I gave Fulton County Family Services all the information to find him including place of employment. There was no word in almost nine years from them! The man was thirty years my senior and had testicular cancer. Believe me when I thought that there was no way that I would get pregnant by him! It didn't matter that he wasn't around! My mother and I took care of Vee for years, and even Bernard helped.

It really hurt that she would think that I wouldn't be there for her. She even gave me another "way out" and said that she would find somewhere to go. I wasn't going to put her out in the cold being pregnant! What kind of person did she think I was?

I didn't even have a second thought about it! I wanted to show her that someone could love her and that I could be her hero and take care of the baby. She had her doubts, and I began to have them as well. We began to sink into bad times again.

We had to move from the apartment on Ashby and began to live in the weekly motels. I had a job at the Atlanta Humane Society, but was having trouble there with a co-worker. *(Just like at Lenox!)*

It amazes me how heterosexual men think that I want their girlfriends! I don't like heterosexual women like that! I am not out for your girlfriend! If she is looking at me, then you are obviously doing something wrong that you need to work on, or you may have a bicurious woman on your hands! That is not my problem. This guy, who was supposed to be my trainer, was a complete jackass that was dating one of the females in the office. I wasn't even thinking about his girlfriend, but I quickly heard that was the reason he was being jerk from another worker.

It turned into a huge problem and eventually I left the job. I couldn't work under those conditions and before it would get "postal", I decided to leave. It wasn't the first time. I had left numerous jobs because of heterosexual men that just couldn't deal with me being me. Most of the women on my job wouldn't mind me being an out butch lesbian. I had only one incident at Telepersonals with a heterosexual woman that treated me differently from everyone else. I think she was just pissed because I showed no interest in her! I can't think of any other reason why it would bother someone so much that I, or someone else, is a homosexual! Unless there are curious feelings, or insecurities inside of that person about homosexuality, then it makes no since to behave that way.

Gail and I were homeless in December 2001. I was in for another revelation at that time. Almost all of the homeless shelters in Atlanta are maintained by churches. There have been numerous complaints about negative treatment of homosexuals and transgender persons in the city.

Gail, being pregnant, was safe as a kitten in the shelter amongst the evangelists, missionaries and pastors! I was still abominable in their site and not worthy of their assistance. My daughters were living with Bernard at the time and my task was to get them to school in the mornings. I had purchased a mint condition station wagon and drove back and forth from East Point to the West End every school day.

The women's day shelter on Ethel Street was where we would go for our meals. It was sad to see so many women and children without places to live. While I was eating, Gail came up and said that some women had invited her to her church. I asked to go, but there was no room on the church bus for me. I stayed at the center until she returned. The women had got her a bed at the Milton Ave shelter for the night. I would spend that evening in my car in the parking lot.

Instead of sleeping, I mostly stayed awake thinking that night. Why was I born a butch lesbian? Yes, I was born a butch lesbian. It was definitely not the life I chose, as some would like to have me think. I wasn't being punished at that time because I was a lesbian. I don't look at my being homeless as a time of punishment at all. I looked at it as another way of seeing how special I actually am. I can't sleep in the shelter. There was no room for me on the church bus. I was an outcast, and so was my Saviour. It was just another task for me to triumph over and praise His name. Moreover, I did.

Gail managed to get me a place to sleep in the Milton Ave shelter that next night. The routine was to go to the day shelter or hang around Woodruff Park in the day, and come back to sleep at night. The homeless men do it as well, but with different shelters. Churches come on buses and pick you up to take you to their building for a meal and a sermon, and then they take you back. One thing about being homeless, I got a lot to eat! Homeless people aren't starving in the city, but they do need a place to stay.

That evening I checked in and showered at the shelter, which used to be a school, with Gail. Since she was pregnant, she got a bottom bunk. I wasn't so lucky and had to scoot my 200 plus pound behind on a top one! I didn't come down the whole evening because I knew it would be a struggle to get back up there!

The next morning I would be kicked out of the Milton Ave shelter. Not because I was a lesbian, but because I had to be a mother! Those shelters have a church member that run the floor in the morning and that person makes out a chore chart for everyone. If you live in the shelter, you have to do a chore or you won't be fed or get your bus tokens. I had to get to East Point early in the morning before Bernard went to work to dress the girls and get them ready for school.

I woke up at 5:00 AM to leave the shelter and the woman wouldn't let me leave. She said that I had to mop the showers or I wouldn't get food or be able to sleep that night.

"If you leave, you can't come back! I don't care what you have to do! There are people waiting on your bed and we have to take care of people that follow the rules!"

I understood the person's position, but getting my children to school was much more important than scooting back up on that top bunk! I was more comfortable sleeping in my car. I told her my choice and I think that I made her mad because she actually wasn't going to let me leave even though I said that I would let go of the bed!

She happened to get a phone call and left me unattended. I quickly rushed out of the fire code doors. By the time she came out just to tell me not to come back, I was already leaving the parking lot in my station wagon to get my daughters!

When it rains it still pours! That evening my station wagon would go kerplunk! There went my transportation *and* my house! Bernard came to get me as I left the car on 14th Street at that Indian restaurant. I'm sure the manager towed it away that evening! Bernard told me that since Gail had a place to stay in the shelter that I could sleep on his couch.

While at Bernard's house, I had a chance to plug up my laptop and start making some money again. I had an idea about a Georgia based business directory and found an investor for it online. I would began designing the website and talking to the person, who lived in up North near Canada.

Gail had our son that January. I was there during delivery and even wore the "father" armband. I bought him a baby book and placed the armband inside the father section for a memory! Gail had moved in with a gay male couple and they were the baby's godparents. I came by three days after he was born to see him and Albert, one-half of the gay couple, said that Gail had gone to the club. Just three days after having the baby, she was out in the cold weather! I told Gail that she would get sick doing that! It was clear that she instantly wanted to get back out into the club scene and didn't care about her health.

I hadn't heard the half of it. Albert was being pressured by his lover to put Gail and the baby out of the apartment. They had given her the master bedroom in the house and were sleeping in their smaller guest room. There was also beginning to be a bond between Gail and Albert that his lover didn't like at all! Albert was the househusband in the relationship and did most of the cooking and cleaning while his partner worked. Those two would be in the house all day with the baby, gossiping, and talking about their mates! That definitely didn't set well with the man of the house and he gave me thirty days to get Gail and the baby out of there!

I was still in talks the investor and he helped me draft up a contract to invest $7,000. He wouldn't be able to send the check for another month and I asked Albert to talk to his mate to stall for a while. Albert would tell me also of a plan that Gail had to give the baby away and that she was secretly dating another woman that worked downtown. I didn't know what to do at that time. I really cared for Gail and our newborn son. This was the chance for us to have a family, and with a new business venture on the horizon, we could start a new life for ourselves.

We couldn't move out of state. Bernard loved the girls and there was no way that I would ever keep a good father like that from seeing his daughter. Gail and I looked at Columbus and Macon for our relocation. I met the lesbian couple that she wanted to take our son just before the check came. I really wondered if Gail was serious, or if she just wanted to push me to make a move. I thought the only reason that she wanted to give him away was because I had carelessly made us homeless. I would have blamed myself if she had given him away.

I had to make a move and I did! When the investor sent the money, I put half into the business, and with the other half, we moved to Conyers, Georgia.

It seemed like the perfect choice. It wasn't too far away for Bernard to visit the girls, and all of Gail's family lived there! In fact, we moved to an apartment complex where her sisters also lived. She finally came out to them, as they would have surely figured it out anyway! Vee and Tee settled into the school system and I felt secure in Conyers. Actually, too secure. The police and sheriff's departments there were relentless, and we had to stay on our p's and q's with auto care and insurance for the mint condition van that we bought.

We were doing so well that Gail invited her adopted family to meet her biological family for her daughter's birthday. I got everything for her daughter's birthday including a Barbie piñata! We invited all the cousins and neighbors and had a grand time. Finally seeing that the both of us were doing well on our own, Gail's adopted mother agreed to let her daughter come live with us! We would now be a family of six!

I had promised Gail that I would help with her daughter's return and I knew that she would be happy. I also had stayed with her throughout the pregnancy and promised her that we would not be homeless again. Maybe I had finally showed her that someone could be there for her, even after she was unfaithful. I thought for sure that she would be in love with me, and we could be happy together.

When Gail's daughter arrived, she was more than ready to spend time with her mother and little brother. She wasn't keen on spending time with my daughters and me. Gail would tell me that her daughter wasn't expecting an instant family and certainly wasn't expecting one with a butch lesbian "father" figure.

"She was mostly expecting to spend more time with me and the baby. I also want her to meet her aunts from Puerto Rico. That's what she was mostly excited for when coming up."

Her daughter's father died just after we started dating. He was Puerto Rican. In fact, just before we moved from Fair Street bottom, he came to see Gail. We were out shopping and had just missed him. Our neighbor said that this tall man came to see Gail and was asking about his daughter. He would have a seizure a few months after that and wouldn't get to see her again. His sisters were always trying to call to see their niece. Gail's adopted mother didn't want them to try to take her daughter, so she would always keep the nieces from seeing her.

No matter what we did, the girls didn't get along. I was seeing my perfect family picture fall to pieces right in front of me. One night, I was listening as Gail's daughter and Vee were talking about fathers and she mentioned that her father was dead. Vee said that she didn't know where her father was and that I was a mother and father figure for her. Vee suggested that she try to look at me as one, too. Her daughter instantly refused.

"Nuh ah! I want a *real* daddy!" she said.

You can't blame a child for that. She was young and had lost her father. We took her to her aunt's house and they gave her a picture of him when he was a little boy. She is his smitten image! That was his daughter and there was no way that I could replace him in her heart even if I'd wanted to. I didn't want to. I just wanted to mean *something* to her. If I had been a biological man then I would have been a hero for bringing her up here with her mother, baby brother and her aunts and throwing a party and everything. However, I felt like I was a fake to her and it meant nothing. It hurt something awful.

Gail still had the ability to meet people and befriended this woman and her husband on the bus. I wouldn't meet the husband until much later, but Tina, his wife would come over to our apartment. They needed a place to stay and Gail would pull some strings to get her an apartment in our building. Tina was a member of The Potter's House Church, and was a self-proclaimed "ex-gay". She said that used to live with her partner and she that she had left her husband to be with the woman. She was also heavily into drugs at the time and had stolen a car. She made a statement that she was *saved* from drugs, stealing—*and* sleeping with women. Now that she was back with her husband, she would try to make Gail leave me and come to her church.

Tina struck a bad cord with me when we met as she took a preference to Gail's daughter over my children. You can hate me all you want, but don't take anything out on my children! It's wrong. Tina would make comments as to Gail's daughter being better than my children because she was half Puerto Rican. They would mostly be about hair and skin tone, and that would tick me off. To compare children like that wasn't even Christian! I quickly told Gail that she wasn't welcomed in my house.

Remember C. Anthony? Well, by that time he wasn't my friend anymore. He had been my best friend for years and we stopped talking because of Gail. He made an obscure sexual comment to me in front of her and she got upset. I told her that I would have him apologize but that wasn't enough for her. She didn't want him to come around us again! Even though he was my friend for many years, because he disrespected her, I wouldn't talk to him or allow him into our house ever again. This was a friend of mine for many years and I tossed him to the side for her.

Do you think that she tossed Tina, whom she had just met on a bus to the side for me?

"This is my house too and she is keeping my daughter for me so she can come over when she wants to! She doesn't have to talk to you and don't have to talk to her!"

Gail knew that I didn't like relationships with people on that note. If I even know you then we are friendly to each other! I don't see how people can be friends with others when they know that they don't get along with their mate or family. Is it just me? I even quit a contracted job that Gail and I had because the person we were working for wasn't please with her performance and chastised her about it.

She was crying after he told her that she wasn't doing a good job and I just couldn't bear it. I don't like to see people cry, especially my girlfriend, or biological men. *(It's just something about seeing bio men cry that gets to me. I really can't explain it)*

I quit a $300 a weekend gig and shunned away one of the best male friends I could have ever had for her—but she chose to keep this woman as a friend over me.

The Marquette was miles down I-20, but was still close enough for Gail. She had learned that she had a bicurious relative and that they both could hang out together. I would spend the first sets of nights at home with the girls and our son. Gail's daughter started spending time over to Tina's apartment when she went out. After I began to complain about her leaving me at home with the baby, she found a babysitter for him with our former proprietor!

There was nothing for me to say now! I had *my* daughters and she had found sitters for *her* children while she went out. Even though we were supposed to be in a partnership and raising a family together, I had no say so over her constant desire to party than to being a parent.

Her daughter's grades were getting horrible in school and Tina wanted to point fingers at me. How? I was hardly spending time with Gail! She was busy going out to the clubs and the bar. Her daughter didn't look to me as anyone important, so how could I be a problem for her schoolwork? She couldn't have thought that Gail loved my daughters or me more because she was hardly ever there!

I couldn't find Gail one night when our son's baby sitter needed her to bring some more diapers. She was out in the van and didn't have a cell phone. I sent Tee to Tina's house to ask if she knew where Gail was. Tina burst into my apartment that night and got into my face.

"Gail left her daughter with me and went out! She saw her ex-boyfriend at work and she probably went to see him. You keep tying her down in this apartment to these kids and trying to be a man! She has someone to take care of her kids so you just take care of yours!"

Tina would also tell me of another time where Gail would tell her that she went out to sleep with a man she met. Her exact words were that she said she had went out and got her some "Good ole dick!"

I was so pissed off that I rented a U-Haul that night and packed everything up. Bernard had one of his friends rent an apartment to me. I left that evening and moved some items into the apartment that Gail didn't know about. I saw that the van was at the mall and took it to help with the rest of the move, since I had to return the U-Haul that morning. I was told that Gail and her relative would be gone for the weekend anyway, so I had time to return the van. Evidently, the weekend fell short as someone called Gail and she heard that I had moved out. Bernard said that she called him.

"Gail said that if you don't back the van, then she will call the police and report it stolen!"

Wasn't that a fine howdy do? I was the one that had paid for the van for Gail, kept it up for her and drove it to Conyers that night after the auction. I was only using it to move the items and was returning it, but she wanted to make it into something more when she is the one that was out cheating! I brought the van back to the mall and caught the bus home. I had a new apartment on the south side of Atlanta in a drug-infested zone. Not good! I wasn't happy at all.

I was so unhappy that I did something that I hadn't done in years. I called that MP chat line and met up with someone! I was lonely and clearly on the rebound, and wanted to go out that night. I met this woman named April and we were supposed to go see Halle Berry's *Gothika* that evening at Magic Theatres.

We ended up only making it to Magic Fridays as she ordered two plates of seasoned meat and rice just for herself! Flashbacks of old times with the briefcase came to mind as I sat with her in the car as she ate and ate and *ate* some more! Her ex-girlfriend would call her about a dozen times that evening and it was just too much for me. I asked her to take me home and she dropped me off at my house. I quickly drifted off to sleep.

I got a call around 4:00 AM from Gail who was at the Marquette Club with her cousin. She asked me where I had been that night. I told her about my date and she said that someone had busted the van's window while she was in the club! *What the heck was she implying?* I don't do crap like that! It reminded me of the bull that Nichelle and Erin said about me vandalizing their cars in Savannah! Gail had parked the van in a darkened area behind the liquor store on Simpson. There were two other vehicles also broken into that evening. I was on a date from hell that night and Miss Karma decided to pay you a visit!

As most lesbian relationships do, Gail and I still dragged it on. It was just too hard out there, and we both knew each other too well to move on. I think it was a little love, but mostly fear on my part. I missed my son and wanted to move back in together. Gail's daughter wasn't happy about us moving back in at all.

We did move back in together at another apartment in Conyers just two months after I moved out. Vee and Tee were also excited about moving back to Conyers with their friends. By then, my apartment rating was shot to hell! I would only be able to move in with private owners or people that gave me a break.

I wanted to make a new mark for myself in business and the gay community. I wanted to trash my old name. I still wanted to be L.A., but I needed a name that would reflect where I'd been, and where I was going.

I was still going to visit Canada one day and wanted to learn French, so I wanted a name that could be interpretive as possibly French or Spanish. I first chose Cervantes, after the playwright for *Man of La Mancha*, my favorite musical! However, I wanted something more original. I would choose JohnTre, because I always said that if I had two boys, then I would name them John and Trevor. Therefore, just before I moved back in with Gail, I told her my new name, *L.A. JohnTre*.

My name would change, but my old skeletons kept following me. I was stopped by the police for a tag violation, and I would spend four days in Conyer's jail. It was for a violation back in Cobb County. It was that ticket I had forgot to pay back when I was dating Nichelle! That was like five years ago and I had a warrant for that and didn't know it! I paid the fine off.

When I went to jail, Gail decided that she would go out to party at the club. She had left my daughters with Tina of all people! I remember coming home from jail that evening and Tina was at the door jeering at me! I didn't think that was cool with her doing that! Going to jail was not a joking matter, even for a traffic violation. It's not like they separate you from the other prisoners that have more violent crimes.

Tina really shouldn't have laughed at me. About a month later, the bondsmen came to pick her up from that stolen car charge. I had spent four days in jail. She would spend about eight months in Covington.

By that time, I had met her husband. He was a nice person and I wondered what he was doing with Tina! He had nowhere to stay while Tina was in jail, and although Gail didn't think it was a good idea, I liked the guy and let him live with us until she got out of jail. While Tina was in jail, she sent letters to Gail and the girls, and even thanked *Gail* for letting her husband stay. I didn't get a letter of thanks. Tina would say that it was just because she and I never really clicked like she did with Gail. Even after her husband told her that it was actually me that let him stay in our house, she still never said anything to me.

Gail took a trip down to South Georgia one time to help a friend of her family's daughter move into a special achievement school. While she was down there another butch lesbian approached her. I didn't hear anything about it, and it was hush-hush amongst the family. At least until Gail planned a trip to go back down there with the friend. I learned from one of them that she went the second time to be with this woman!

Someone had tipped her off that I knew about the meeting and she came back waiting on me to say something. This would be the third or fourth sign of infidelity from Gail. I didn't even confront her about it because I was just too used to it. It seemed that she wanted to fight or argue. I think Gail always wanted to get into a confrontation with me and I always avoided it. I just don't have it in me to fight and argue. It's ignorant to me.

Well, will there be something good coming out of this move to Conyers? I tried to apply for government assistance again for Vee and got a letter from Rockdale County Child Support. They said that a judge in Florida wanted swab samples from Vee and me to do a paternity test! After 12 *years* of nothing in Fulton County, it took only 60 *days* in Rockdale County to track down William! He didn't even remember who I was! The paternity test proved that he was Vee's father and he instantly started sending support for her. He was actually happy to have a daughter, and I was happy for Vee to be able to have a relationship with him as well. All of my baby change was now accounted for!

Gail would also have contact with our son's bio father. She had started letting him stay weekends with several people and one of them would take him to see his bio dad. We moved to Lithonia, (where I would finally make a home), and Gail would let her kids leave to stay with other people more than they would be with us.

One time her daughter went to stay with her aunts. She wrote letters to her, our son and the girls saying how she missed them all while she was gone. You guess it—she wrote nothing to me! Her daughter just didn't think of me as anything, and I was the one that helped her get to see her aunts. I was upset and Gail wanted to fight about it.

"I can't make my daughter like you! She is a child and she doesn't know that you were the one that bought her all those gifts and helped her get up here! She doesn't have to like you. We are forcing this lifestyle on her that she doesn't understand!"

I had no idea why she was even talking to me. I didn't say anything about her daughter at all. You could tell that I was disappointed. I really cared for her daughter, and it hurts when you care about someone—especially a child—and they don't love you back. I didn't say anything though. I just walked away in disgust. Before I could reach the door to leave, Gail pushed me.

My daughters were crying in the background asking us not to fight. I told them that I wasn't fighting and to calm down.

"Gail, I am not going to fight you! You have wanted me to fight you for years and I am not going to do that! I'm not that other guy. I'm sorry. If you don't want me, then fine. I care about your daughter and yes, it hurts that she thinks nothing of me, but I am not mad at her or you about it! I'm hurt, but not mad."

Gail then said something that matched the pain of when her daughter said that she wanted a *real* daddy.

"You aren't that other guy because you aren't a guy! You're a *wannabe*."

Ouch. That's just not something you say to the butch that you are in a relationship with! *(Now that I think about it. It was even more painful!)*

I got a call from one of the aunts asking when Gail was going to send her daughter's information, so that they could get her in school. I was told that she was only staying two weeks, but obviously, Gail had decided to do what her adopted mom had feared that she would do.

She was giving her daughter to the aunts. I had no say so in the matter. Even though we were in a partnership, she still considered them as *her* children, including the son we had together.

She was even considering giving him to the lesbian couple that had wanted him when he was a newborn. They argued that he should have a relationship with his father, and that he should not have even have called me "Daddy", as he did for his first years of life.

I would also find some messages on my computer where Gail was online and talking to people in a message board chat. She was saying that she had always found femmes more attractive and that she feels that she has always been butch. She further went on to tell those people that one time, when she was out with me, there was a femme that she really wanted to talk to, but she couldn't because she was with me! She then said that she wanted to leave me but she didn't want to break my heart.

She knew that she had wasted the last two years of her life with this "stud" that she really didn't want! She just didn't know how to leave me! I didn't confront her about these messages either. She never knew that I had read them.

(There was no point in her wasting more time with me.)

I decided to help Gail out. I stopped paying rent at the apartment where we were living. I had the money, but I just didn't want to pay it. I was tired and told Gail that we needed to be looking for a place to stay.

I told Gail that Bernard got me and the girls an apartment in the same complex, but that she couldn't stay with me because he didn't like her. Which he didn't. In fact, I don't think any of my ex-girlfriends fared well with him, especially after the Nichelle episode!

I took the girls and we settled into a two-bedroom apartment. I gave Vee and Tee the bedrooms and I took a blow up mattress and claimed the living room! After staying with Gail when she cheated on me and got pregnant; helping her bring her daughter up here, only for her to not like me and be given away to the aunts; being called a *wannabe*, and—me being in the way when she wanted to talk to someone else—that was enough. We all get tired some time and I was exhausted! That was 4 years of my life, and my longest relationship—male or female.

Unfortunately, I would also have to let our son go. After the lesbian couple let him meet his bio father, he came to see me. He saw a person that resembled him, and ran after him calling him, Daddy. I had to apologize to the stranger, and explain to him that he was not his father, and he started crying. For the first time since birth, I was now just "L.A." in his eyes.

That was another hard pill to swallow. Gail to this day just doesn't understand why I had to forget him. It's the pain. Sometimes it's best to just forget. He would never know me as who I was ever again. Why would I continue to hurt myself like that?

He is not living with Gail as I write this. He is living with another family, and gets to visit his sister from time to time. It's what Gail felt was best for him as his mother, and that is all that matters.

Chapter 15

Life Changing Love

"Yolanda"
(2004)

I did have a little assistance moving away from Gail. I had logged on to a popular lesbian website and met a mixed raced woman in Virginia named Yolanda. She was just what I was looking for as far a romantic and diverse. She spoke fluent Spanish and had two young children.

Yolanda would write me haikus and little, romantic love notes that I hadn't received in years! She was also very feminine and loved to shop! I hate to admit it, but I really love to go shopping with women. Maybe that estrogen in me enjoys walking around a store with another woman! I don't have to buy anything myself, neither does she, but I enjoy watching a woman try on shoes, clothes and can spend hours doing it!

Yolanda and I would keep contact long enough for me to be motivated to leave Gail. She had her own problems in Virginia. Her ex-husband would constantly come over to her home while she was talking to me over the phone. He still had a key to the house. I guessed later that it was because it was still *his* house!

She worked as personal assistant for another man. She had to buy his clothes for and keep his books in order. He would also call her at all times of the night. She also had a butch ex-girlfriend that was constantly stalking her. All of this and the fact that she lived miles away from me wasn't too intriguing.

I had planned to come visit her as soon as I settled the girls into our new apartment. I lost touch with her for a week because of what she said were relatives coming over to her house. It turns out that during that week she met someone else from the same website and they were coming to see her. She told me that whoever got to her first would be whom she would start a relationship with.

I had wrote her a song that I was going to serenade her with, and even put up a cute website for her, but she wasn't enough for me to go off to the races against another butch.

She had also become quite mean to me! I had just left a woman that was very mean to me, and couldn't stand that! *Adios!*

I never had a chance to meet her, but I named my web hosting business after her so that I could make use of the domain I purchased for her website!

(After 5 years, the briefcase was back! I dropped in a haiku!)

When I first saw the briefcase during the move, I quickly opened it and found Nichelle's old love letter. The vial I placed in the bag gave the letter her scent that I remembered. That letter was now almost ten years old! I had been with Gail all that time and was never truly in love with her.

I had only loved one person up until that point and that was Nichelle. Had I learned anything from my domestic partnership or those ten years of dating? I really hadn't. The harshest lessons in my life were about to be learned. I had been craving love and romance and even a simple kiss for years! I was live bait for any woman that showed me a little affection, and I was about to be bitten by a shark.

"Lauralee"
(2004 – 2005)

Just before the end of the 2004 holiday season, I developed an interest in astrology. I thought that I could use it to get a little help in finding a good mate for me. After some research, I found out that Tracy, Devonne and Nichelle were all born under the sun sign of Gemini! I am a Leo sun sign and a Gemini is a good match for me on some charts. I found out that Gemini women are very intellectual and diverse, which is probably why I have been so attracted to them. Digging deeper into the chart and being a Leo-Dog, Nichelle was the perfect match of one of my soul mate's combinations, a Gemini-Cat. *Interesting! My perfect match left me stranded in Savannah!*

I got back on a chat line and met a Gemini-Ox from Alabama named Lauralee. She had answered my ad a few times, and gave me a certain time to call her, but I could never get through. It wasn't until I realized that Alabama time was one hour off Georgia time, that I found out I wasn't calling her when she had asked me to! She was another woman that had a rough marriage. She said that she was sure that she wanted to meet a "man that was *not* a man". Just what I was looking for!

We would talk both at her job and while she was at home. I used to call her at her lunchtime and we'd chat. I told her about the incident with Nichelle and about my failed partnership with Gail and that's never a good thing to do. I always give out too much information when meeting someone and trying to start something with them. *Thank goodness, I won't have to do that anymore! I'll just give them a copy of this book!*

Lauralee was extremely sweet and I loved her voice. She had a way of saying things that my ears weren't used to. I longed for some sweetness in my life and Lauralee gave that to me.

I was even more excited when I found out that Lauralee was moving to Georgia soon. I had always wanted to be the tour guide and help my mate move. I guess that I've always had that lesbian U-Haul dream! We both agreed that we wanted mates that had their own place. We would have probably repeated that *Brady Bunch* episode if we attempted to move in together since she had three boys! I also don't want to go through that "I want a *real* daddy" thing ever again!

I had emailed my pictures to Lauralee days after we started talking. It was the same photos that I took for Yolanda's website and CD cover, but she didn't know that! I've shopped those photos around the internet for years now. I told her that everyone said that I looked like *Theo* from the Cosby Show in those shots and she agreed. I wonder if Malcolm Jamal-Warner knows that he has a lesbian that could have doubled for him?

Lauralee didn't have any pictures online, so she had her son take a few and sent them to me with this letter. She made me promise not to look at the pictures before I read the letter and I kept it!

January 12, 2005
Wed 6:00 PM

Hi Sweetie! (Smiley Face)

Well, I'm here! As you know by now I pretty much <u>HATE</u> nearly every one of these pictures. (Frowny Face)...But enough chit chat!

(She explained all 7 of the pictures she sent here. I thought she was quite attractive. She always thought she was fat for some reason.)

Okay..with the good or bad, for the most part this is me. I refused to send you the ones where I really looked like a hippo! These I look...chunky. Keep in mind (I keep telling myself) I was on and swollen and bloated..yeah, okay. That'll work...(Smiley Face). Anyway, if you can, enjoy the pictures! Okay. Yeaa (Smiley Face) Lauralee.

P.S. I didn't sign love or smooches because I may not be your cup of tea. If I'm not then I figured that not having to deal with love/smooches would make it easier for you to say so...That was one of the reasons that I didn't want you to tell me about the big butt, big breasted version/image you had of me...Soooo not me!!! (Frowny Face) Anyway, I'm ending here. I want to say that I really appreciate you...for being you and being you for me. Sincerely, Lauralee.

I don't know what gave Lauralee the impression that I wanted the big-butt, big-breasted type of woman anyway. That was not my type at all. Besides, I was still on my inside matters outlook and didn't really care what Lauralee looked like.

Lauralee drove up with her sons to meet me just days after I got the letter. I was frantically searching for a gift for her. I wanted to bring her some flowers or a teddy bear to mark our first meeting, but I couldn't find anything. We met in the West End and hopped aboard the MARTA train to go downtown. It was her first time on the train and she was scared to death at the motion. She held my hand the entire time. It was very cute to me!

We enjoyed time at Underground Atlanta with the kids that day. That evening, we found ourselves in just each other's company. After a night of intimacy, I asked Lauralee if she wanted to continue our relationship and she said that she did!

All was well between us until I got an unusual request from one of my neighbors. I lived two units away from a lesbian couple that were having relationship problems. I had become an acquaintance of the butch because she was a member of my Yahoo group.

She asked me to place and ad for her in my group so that she could find another friend. She knew that her girlfriend would check her email so she asked me to use mine instead of hers for responses. This was a bad idea on several accounts! One was that I was assisting someone with cheating on their girlfriend! However, the biggest oversight was that I had forgotten that Lauralee had also joined my Yahoo group!

I placed the ad and Lauralee saw it. She didn't say anything to me about it until after she came back from shopping with a friend. I spent the whole evening trying to explain to her what had happened! I even had the butch call her and explain the whole thing! She wasn't hearing her or me and was very upset.

She had lost all respect for me then, but she said that she had forgiven me. She said so, but I don't think she ever did. I would notice many changes in her over the next few weeks. She had even returned to the chat line.

Lauralee told me that she would always leave a relationship first and that the other person would stay even though she had given up on it. I really didn't want to give up so soon and tried everything I could to have her trust me again.

Lauralee would need help with the move and she would contact me with questions. She also needed financial support and I offered to e-file her income tax refund. I was still doing those for people for additional income and I wanted to show her that she could trust me.

She received the refund and made a trip to Georgia, but not to see me. She came to house hunt and to visit another friend that she had met before me. It seemed as though I couldn't do anything right by her and although she never admitted it, I could tell that she had started another relationship with someone.

I had feelings for Lauralee that were similar to what I had felt for Nichelle. I was in love with Lauralee, and she had tossed me to the side because she thought I was being unfaithful to her. What I did for my neighbor was stupid, but I didn't want to lose the love of my life for it!

There was another incident where Lauralee thought that I had mentioned another woman's name during one of our conversations. I really didn't, but she just didn't trust me. She was the only woman that I wanted. I couldn't convince her of that and I didn't think that she wanted me too. Just before her move date, I called to ask when she wanted me to rent the U-Haul for her. That was our initial plan.

"That won't be necessary, now. I have friend of the family that is helping me", she said.

I wanted to come and see her for her birthday just before the move and she gave me a pity speech.

"You are such a great person, and if I don't see all of the good things in you that you have to offer, then that is my loss!"

My butch neighbor, who was at first apologetic, said that this was bull! She said that Lauralee wanted a way out of our relationship anyway and asked me to think about it more.

"If Lauralee had been in love with you as you said she was, then even when you did that for me she would not just jump back on a chat line and start going right back out to meet people! She didn't want to be with you moving to the ATL! This is a Black lesbian paradise and you don't bring sand to the beach!"

I admit that didn't make me feel much better at all. I felt horrible and I blamed myself for her leaving me. She moved to Georgia and didn't talk to me very much at all at first. Finally, we went out on a date to see *Mr. & Mrs. Smith* when on its opening day at the mall.

Lauralee would later call it an *outing* and wouldn't even hold my hand. She kept checking her cell phone for someone else to call while we were together. She would even end the night with a hug and tell me that she always hugged her *friends*.

It was a déjà vu for me, as it resembled the *outing* I had with Nichelle to Savannah. It was the same results. I was in love with someone that didn't care for me anymore. By the middle of the year, Lauralee had stopped contacting me altogether.

I started to hate the idea of relationships, and dating, and domestic partnerships and just decided that I would do something else.

I began an online reseller business with seven other investors late 2005 and tried to make money to get my mind off being in love with Lauralee. It was a great idea and we accumulated over $15,000 to support the new company in just two months. I wanted to keep myself as busy as possible. I didn't use the chat line where I met Lauralee because she was still on there and hearing her ads depressed me. I didn't go back on the lesbian website or the message boards. I was losing my faith in those, and finding the woman for me.

Gail would contact me just before I started the new company with a request. By that time, both of her children were living with other people, and she was in between jobs. She was pregnant again and needed somewhere to stay. At this time, she was even a self-proclaimed butch!

It seems that some butches get pregnant more than femmes, doesn't it? Oh well, we are *men* with *wombs*, right?

Tee volunteered her bedroom for Gail to sleep until she had her third child. We would be great friends for each other during these times. I would be there when she had her second son. There still would be no father, but there would be a lot of love and support. She would give custody of this child to my ex-sister-in-law at birth.

Chapter 16

Triple Threat Weekend,
Not Black Enough & The Truth

My business venture would be in the red the first of the year 2006, and would falter, as we would lose all of our accounts and bank backing. I would have to find something else to occupy my time again. I was *untouchable* in the romance department. I had given the chat lines a serious break and had stopped dating. I was miserable!

Lauralee had been my last relationship and I was still thinking about her on a daily basis. It took me a few months to get over Nichelle, but Lauralee was a life changing love for me. I didn't cheat on Lauralee at all, but she thought that I did, and I felt like I had lost my soul mate because of a stupid mistake. I had to do something to ease my pain and I didn't feel like writing back then!

"Triple Threat Weekend"
January 13th – January 16th 2006

After an 8-month dating hiatus, I decided to try the chat line again and setup three dates during the M.L. King Holiday weekend. I hardly even remember these women's real names, so I won't even bother making up any for them! I didn't save anything for the briefcase either!

That Friday night I met this woman in Alpharetta. She told to arrive at her place around 8:00 PM. I like being punctual so I got there at about 7:45PM. She was upset that I arrived so "early" and asked me to wait in the parking lot until she was ready. I sat out there until about 8:20PM.

I was just about to drive off when she finally came to the door! She described herself perfectly, and was a nice dresser. We went to my first ever visit to a Japanese hibachi grill restaurant. The evening was perfect as she re-introduced me to sushi and sake. *(I love a woman that can get into some sushi!)*

The only flaw to that first date was that something made me sick that night. I couldn't stop coughing after we left the restaurant! Now, here we were back at her house and I couldn't make any moves on her because I was coughing! She was very health conscious and didn't want to catch anything from her date, of course!

She was cordial enough to watch a movie while I held her. I was just too embarrassed to stay after the movie, so I left! She would call me the next day to check on me. I didn't cough anymore after I left her house. We were supposed to arrange another date after that but I never heard from her again. I must've been allergic to her or something! Oh well, one down—two to go!

That Saturday night would have me in East Point. I picked this woman up that still lived with her parents. She seemed ok, but reminded me of Bridgett after we got to the restaurant! She used to date a chef so she was very meticulous about her food and constantly reordered plates. We would go to see a movie after dinner. She was one of those folks that loved to talk during the movie and I can't stand that! This time it was her that would get sick and start coughing on the date!

I was bored with her and wanted to take her home when she suggested that we go to Phaze 1. That was a nice drive and actually closer to my house! I didn't want to be a bad date, so I took her there. After we got there, she appeared to be looking for someone that night. *Oh no, was I about to be a mark to make someone jealous, again?*

She got on the dance floor and asked me to hold her purse! What? You wanted to dance alone? It was definitely time to drop her off! We finally left the club and I took her back to her parent's house. She started coughing again when she exited the car. I laughed under my breath! *Don't worry sister! I don't want a kiss from you, either! Farewell!*

It was now Sunday and I'm thinking that this date would be better than the other two! No coughing and no clubbing! This was a settled, much older woman that owned her home and was a fellow entrepreneur like me. I was bound to have fun with her. It couldn't get any worse, right?

This woman had a peculiar voice. She could have been a voice double for Eartha Kitt! I could almost hear her *growling* through the phone as she spoke! Still, I wasn't the least bit worried about meeting her.

I drove to her house in East Atlanta around that evening. It was nice. You could tell it was freshly built. East Atlanta was another one of those neighborhoods in a rebuilding process. You would see a nice house nestled in between two or three abandoned homes. This was the case with my date. You'd thought the entire street was deserted until you got to her house!

I sat in the car and prepared myself. Brushed my teeth and dabbed some cologne. I noticed that she was peeking through an upstairs window. *Trying to catch a sneak preview, are we?*

She must be one of those women that if the blind date didn't look good she wouldn't answer the door. I wasn't discouraged at all! I got out of the car in my two-piece suit and favorite Calvin Kline black trench coat. Fresh breath, fresh hairdo, Lagerfeld cologne and a Chrysler 300 rental luxury sedan! What, me worry?

When she opened the door, she was not what I had pictured! She put you in the mind of Iman, the fashion model from the eighties. However, she was much larger! I was not concerned with her looks. I was interested in the fact that she liked sushi and had an interest in fine wine. She had visited some California vineyards and I told her that was something that I would like to do.

She showed me some wine books while she mixed her a drink. I had really stopped drinking so I just had some juice. It was another change after Lauralee. I just didn't like drinking beer or alcohol as much anymore. A friend would say later that I was still in a deep depression.

We went to this Sushi bar on Ponce de Leon in Midtown. We ordered sushi and got the traditional Japanese customary herb soup. I was wondering why it was taking a long time for the sushi to arrive after I had finished my soup.

My date would tell me that it was because I still had my bowl in front of me! Ok? So they look at that? Apparently, because just as soon as I placed the soup bowl to the side the server brought our sushi! I would even learn from her how to mix the ginger and the wasabi paste for each bite! Delicious! I know a lot about computers and running a business, but this was the stuff I wanted to learn! Different food and cultures! This woman was looking quite promising.

She ordered our wine by year and type, and whatever else you are suppose to when you know what you are doing! At first she asked me to do it, which I adored that in her! A man usually does that on a date. As I've mentioned, butch lesbian roles are as close to a heterosexual man that you can get, and although we don't want to be looked on in society as "man wannabes", we get some pleasure when our mates allow us to have those moments. Clearly, she understood the honor that would give me on a butch-femme date. Unfortunately, I was unable to order and asked her to do so until she taught me how to distinguish the wines!

We had great conversation and I drank about a half of a glass of the $80 bottle of wine she ordered. I was driving and I asked her to enjoy it. Eventually, she did drink the rest of the bottle! We sat at the bar for more conversation and she ordered another drink. If you've been counting then you'll know that's a third of a bottle of wine, plus two cocktails counting the one she had before we left. I suggested that we go to the restaurant near the Fox that plays live jazz, but she insisted that I take her back to her house.

I noticed that she was getting a little more talkative on the way back to her house. She asked me what I did, why was I single, and on that chat line!

She then echoed my friend's conversation at the Otherside some years back and said that no one without problems would be on that chat line! Ok. I just met *you* from that chat line that you are putting down! What gives?

"I just don't like the people on there" she said. "They are liars and cheaters! They always lie to you! When I heard your voice then I thought you were an ugly liar too! That is why I looked out the window to see what you looked like first! You are not ugly and in fact I like the way you look!"

Ok. Thanks.

We arrived at her house and she invited me in. I wanted to talk to her more, so I came in and sat down on her couch. She asked me for my coat and to take off my shoes. Something about the rugs in the living room, she said. So, I did!

She quickly went into the kitchen and fixed two vodka and soda drinks complete with lime. I was definitely dealing with a woman that knew her liquor! She offered me a drink in which I cordially refused.

"I'm sorry. I have to drive home tonight and I live way in Dekalb County."

She gave me a look that I clearly read as she was surprised that I *wanted* to go home that night! I think she wanted to score with me, so I did what most men or butches would do in that situation. I took the drink!

She gave me another wine book to look at while she refreshed her glass, *again*. I got a phone call from the office while she was in the kitchen. It was Gail, who was my office manager at that time. She was at the office and was about to leave in an hour, so she asked if I wanted to hang out with the crew. It was one of the only times my employees would ask me to go out with them!

I told Gail that I couldn't because I was on a date. She seemed upset about that and hung up the phone without saying goodbye.

(I didn't understand why she did that.)

My date came back and wanted to know whom I was talking to. I told her about my ex-partner working for my company, and that she just had a general office question. She mumbled something at first, and then just became quiet as she gulped down her new glass. The count is now at a third of a bottle of wine, a mixed unknown and four vodka and soda cocktails.

She asked to refresh my glass and this time I firmly refused. I knew that I had more than enough to drink. I also now realized that I was dealing with a woman with a drinking problem and had to be sober enough to drive home! She grabbed the glass out of my hand and ripped open my shirt! It was not the fantasy that I'd always had of that happening, and it didn't turn me on at all! I was getting quite scared. She jumped on top of me and kissed me hungrily. My mind went racing!

Ok. You are in this woman's house and she is obviously horny and drunk! You've been in a bad "marriage" for four years with one woman, and broken hearted for the last year by another! Maybe this is something you need to pick you up! A night of lustful, drunken, uninhibited sex! Besides, you just paid $150 for wine and dinner! You deserve it on several counts!

I snapped out of it—or I should say was *slapped* out of it by my date at that moment!

"You are a liar! I hate when people lie to me! That car outside is a rental car! It has too many miles on it to be yours and a 2006! You just flashed money at me, gave me this idea that you didn't know anything about wine and sushi, and wanted to learn so I would feel sorry for you and give you my body! You knew about all of these things! Then, your girlfriend called and she works for you! What a lie!"

If she had just asked me about the car then I would have told her that it was a rental anyway, while she was looking at the odometer and playing detective! I really didn't know anything about wine, or eating sushi correctly, and Gail did actually worked for me! As for the sex part, I was in a drought, but perfectly fine! But, no use of trying to explain myself! I was ready to get out of there. Before I could get up, she apologized.

"Wait. Stay the night with me. I'll get you another drink. You lied but you are a good one and you have soft, juicy kissable lips! You have earned some from me!"

I've *earned* some? Well, goody-goody for me! I also finally get a compliment on my big lips and it's from a woman with a blood alcohol level the size of both of Shaq's shoes put together!

I went into her bathroom and quickly tried to call Gail at the office. She answered and I whispered the situation to her. She hung up on me! She just didn't care that I was being held hostage!

(What was up with her that night?)

I had decided to leave and could get to my shoes but my trench coat was in her bedroom closet! I had placed my wallet in my shoes so I decided to just leave the $300 coat behind! She called me into the kitchen as I was about to make a dash for it.

Damn! The keys to the rental car were in my trench coat! I couldn't leave. I met her in the kitchen and sat at the counter. She was gulping down yet another drink!

"I changed my mind she said," she said. "You are cute but I still don't like liars! Get out of my house!"

I asked for my coat and she pointed me to her bedroom closet. I swiftly ran in there to get it but was closely followed by her. She gave me a swipe on the behind and laughed as I exited the room!

I thought I'd better hurry out of there before she changed her mind again! She had a few more harsh words to say while I was on her porch.

"You thought you were very slick tonight, didn't you? If you owned a business then you would have offered me a card!"

Since I was safely on the porch in my coat and shoes, I reached into my wallet and pulled out one of my business cards for her.

"I don't want your fake card! Get off of my porch!"

I threw up my hands and walked away. I could hear her slam her door behind me. I breathed a sigh of relief as I slowly approached my car. She had gone upstairs and I could still hear her calling me a fake and a liar through the open window. Before I got in, she appeared in the bedroom window and asked me to wait again because she was coming down!

I turned the key, back out of her driveway, and sped through the streets of East Atlanta, hitting I-20 at 60MPH, and didn't stop until I was in Lithonia!

The next day, she called me while I was working. She asked me if I had enjoyed myself that evening and if I wanted to go out again soon.

She had no idea of what happened that evening! I just told her that she had a "really bad night" and that I wouldn't be going out with her again. I also wished her the best and hoped that she could see her drinking problem soon.

In April of 2006, I was still trying to get over my traumatic experience with the vodka-drinking woman in East Atlanta. I had stopped dating again and through myself into my work. To my surprise, I got an email from Lauralee! I really hadn't heard very much from her since she moved to Georgia. She wanted to know how I was doing and asked about the girls. She also mentioned how much she wanted to see me again and that she may have to "marry me this time around!"

I admit that I was still in love with her! I was still blaming myself that we weren't together. Seeing her email was wonderful and I was ready to see her again, too! I wanted this woman anyway. This was the second woman that I ever fell in love with and I was getting a chance to be with her again.

We continued to talk and I did get to see Lauralee again that June. I bought us some tickets to the Gerald Levert and Kelly Price play, *Confessions* at the Fox Theatre. It's a good thing we went to see them too, because Gerald would pass away just 4 months later of a heart attack.

We had a great dinner, saw the play and even had a drink later. I was happy to be out with her again! However, it would end on a sour note!

Even though it was a date, Lauralee treated it the same way as she did the last one that we had almost a year earlier. She just wanted to get out of the house! I didn't even get a goodnight kiss from her!

She would insist that she went with me as a *friend* and not a date! BS! I treated her like a lady and paid for everything! Butches and men don't do that as friends, especially not to women that they have been intimate with and are obviously in love with. Lauralee played that friend card just because she thought I would buy that because I was still a woman. There is no way that she plays that card on a man! It's easier to play on a butch!

I was in my car crying that night after that! I hadn't cried in months over her or anyone else. She even had the audacity to say that I should go back to "doing whatever I was doing before she emailed me again".

Who really was this woman really that I fell in love with and was pining over for a year? Was it *really* my fault that she left?

Not Black Enough

"The Red-Haired Lady"
(2006)

I was going back into that depressed stage again after that date with Lauralee. I just didn't want to believe that she was suckering me! Could she be doing as Nichelle did? They were both Gemini women! Nevertheless, I love Gemini women! That could be one of my problems.

I wanted to take my mind off Lauralee. I decided to go out to a club alone. I hadn't done that in years! I even decided to go to a different club than I usually attend. I went to My Sisters Room in Decatur. This was a great spot for acoustic lesbians! I got there and as I expected, there was only about three Black lesbians in the whole place. I was somewhat excited to be in a different atmosphere for a change and the women were nice there! Especially the bartender, who bought me cokes all nights, after I told her I didn't drink alcohol while out alone.

I sat close to the stage, as it was a night where they were recording artists for their CD's. I listened to several women, mostly butch, come up and perform original ballads. I was so into the music that I didn't notice the women sitting next to me. One of them was a red haired lady that I thought was a butch. She leaned over to me and asked me if that was my first time in My Sister's Room.

"No, I've been her before on other nights. Just not karaoke or open mic!"

I had only been to MSR when they had hip-hop nights or special events. It wasn't a place that I went to frequently at all. I was a veteran of the old MSR that was in Midtown because it was next to Duprees where Marie and I used to shoot pool. I didn't come as much when they moved to Decatur.

I would always say that the music was great and that the setup was spectacular with the gazebo garden and the Elvis mural trailer. It looked like they had taken someone's house and made it into a party spot! The dance floor was in the driveway of the place and the stage was damn near on the railroad tracks! Still, the place rocked and I liked the people!

The red haired lady was a guest of one of the musicians and I thought that she would make a great friend. I think that is just what I needed instead of a girlfriend. She told me that her and her friends played cards on certain nights and loved to barbecue. I was down for that so I asked her for her number.

She went to get some paper to write down her number. Her friend leaned over to me and said that they were like sisters that looked out for each other so that I need to make sure that I was cool. Ok? What the heck was she talking about? I just wanted to come over for card night!

When the red head lady came back she sat next to me and put her arms around me! I was shocked! I thought she was a butch. I wasn't trying to talk to her like that! Oh, no! I've screwed up again! What do I do? She asked for a drink and I bought one for her. After the last set, I excused myself and left the club. She said that she'd call me to make sure I got home safely.

While driving home I was as confused as ever. I had never dated a Caucasian woman before. It's not that I don't, in fact I was almost introduced to a Caucasian woman by an employee of mine earlier in the year.

"You said that Black women have a problem with your big lips! White women would love them! You should try dating out of your race for a change. You are not going to find too many Black women that like sushi and going to operas and plays like you do! You need to do like the straight brothers do and get you a White woman!"

This came out of the mouth of a Black gay man in case you wanted to know! It's not the first time that I was told that I should try interracial dating. I'd only dated Black and one Puerto Rican woman up until that point, and it would be a change. But wait! I didn't want to date the red haired lady just because she was

White! I'd just wanted to be her friend anyway. I had to see what type of personality that she had so I told her about my past relationships. Again, that's a big mistake no matter what the race!

"It seems like you have had women run over you because you are nice. I had the same type of abuse from my ex-girlfriend. She used to beat me and we would fight about anything!"

We talked for hours that evening. It felt good to talk to someone, rather than wait for Lauralee to call or email me. I had grown to like my red haired new friend. I call her that simply because she emphasized it so much, especially during the first time that we were intimate.

She said that the way to tell if you are dating a true redhead, is that the hair would be red in both places—if you catch my drift! I wonder if that theory works with true blonde-haired women, too?

She asked me to come out to her apartment and spend some time with her. I made the drive to Gwinnett to see her. She got me interested in her, and the Harry Potter series, that same day! I thought that maybe I could have something with her.

She lived with her friend that I'd met that night. Her roommate had a girlfriend that the red haired girl couldn't stand! She used to get really theatrical about it too. At first, I paid it no mind, but it started to get crystal clear. She liked her friend that she was living with, and I was just a mark to make the friend jealous! (Déjà vu like a mother!)

But, there was even more to the story. She had dated another Black butch that the friend didn't like at first. This butch was more gangster Black and rugged, and took her to get her nails done. The roommate described her as treating the red haired lady like a "chickenhead", and she was obviously going to be abusive to her.

While riding with her in my car we would sing Maroon 5 songs and listen to alternative music. She asked me if I like country music and I said yes, some of it. She told me that she never really met a Black butch like me and that she didn't know how to deal with it. I bought her some flowers one day and she told me that she was talking back with the other Black butch that took her to the mall and that was more gangsta!

Oh for the love of...! How in the hell did I let this happen to me? I tried to talk to a woman outside of my race for the first time, that I didn't even want to talk to in the first damn place, and she dumps me because I am not Black enough for her!

Isn't that the same stereotypical BS that exists in the heterosexual community that all White women want to be with bad, gangsta Black men? Bite the <bleep> out of my ass!

(For the record, I won't take what this red haired woman did to me as indication that all White femme lesbians that date Black butch lesbians want them to be gangstas and kick their ass!)

The Truth

After I was dumped for my lack of Blackness, I started back communicating with Lauralee. I had done some things for the red haired lady like invited her over to my house and pampered her a bit and Lauralee acted like she was kind of upset.

She also admitted that there were four other women that were interested in her, but that I was in her "top two" persons of interest. That was good to know, I think?

She then brought back up the red haired lady and asked if I had slept with her.

"Yes, but what difference does it make? You could care less who I sleep with, Lauralee!" I was serious about that statement. She hadn't given me any indication that she gave a hoot!

"Yes, I do care", she said.

Wow, I didn't know. I was pleased to hear it, but shocked. I had wanted to hear it for over a year!

I asked her to come spend some time with me. I told her to bring the boys and even their dog to stay with the girls and me. She came on two occasions and one time even stayed four days with me. I kept her in my bed and arms as much as I could.

I even took her to Phaze 1 and she danced all night long. I stood there watching her body sway. She was beautiful! I was with the woman that I was in love with and would do anything for her again!

After the first time she stayed with me, I went to Stonecrest Mall to find a copy of Phyllis Hyman's *Old Friend*. The song fit us because of the situation and it played while we were making love on the second visit. I had made a mistake, but my soul mate came back to me. I never cheated on her at all, but what I did by trying to help someone cheat was just as wrong. I had regained her trust and a special place in her heart.

(Hold that thought for a moment.)

Do you remember the *Peanuts* gang? Almost every episode would start with that <bleep>, Lucy holding that football for Charlie Brown to kick, and just when he was about to kick it—that <bleep> would move the football out of the way! For years I'd watched that cartoon, and even one time the <bleep> said that she wouldn't move the %^&! football! One time, she even *promised* him that she wouldn't move the %^&! football! But sure enough, when he ran to kick it, the <bleep> moved the !*&^ damn ball just like always! I even wrote a letter to the comic strip creator, Charles Schultz when I was little. Just once, I asked him! Please, let him kick it—or at least miss and hit the <bleep> in the face or something! He never answered my letter, and he died years ago. Charlie Brown never got to kick that football!

(Damn. Will I ever get to kick it?)

Lauralee stopped calling me again for a few days and I went into a state of flux. I kept contacting her with texts and she just said that she was going into one of her Gemini mood swings. She used to email me every day and she stopped, but she would be online chatting on Yahoo. I would read her net blog and find out that she was flirting with someone online, had phone conversations and was planning to meet them.

She had never *said* that we were back together, but she came over to my house and stayed there. We both said that we don't have casual sex, or sex with people that we don't care about! Lauralee was at my house for days and we had plenty of non-casual sex! I had even started to help her pay her cable bills and had access to her personal account information. She trusted me with all that and still we weren't in a relationship? What was going on?

I came online one evening and she had her "Do Not Disturb" icon on with a message that she was "SO not online right now". I was such a chump! Can you imagine how that felt? I was the mark that had paid the damn Internet bill that she was using to chat with this person on!

I got an email that her Internet service was going to be disconnected if she didn't make another payment but I didn't tell her. She was SO not online to talk to me, so I was SO not going to let her make a fool of me anymore! The phone went off and she had her son call to ask me for some money to help pay it. What nerve!

I knew the truth then! I was sucker before, too. I realized that she might have never loved me. Either that or she started using me after she thought I cheated on her! To think that I spent a year of my life hurting and crying out for her, when all the while she could care less how I felt.

She eventually got the phone back on and called me. I didn't answer. She tried once more the next evening and couldn't get me. The last words I would hear her say were "Never mind", on my answering machine. I fought myself for days from calling her and went into some serious withdrawal.

Nevertheless, I knew that after I finally listened to the "truth", then I would feel better. My love for her was true and I never cheated. It wasn't my fault that Lauralee left me. I had punished myself undeservingly for over a year.

Chapter 17

Let Me Show You Something

My older brother, Perry was being evicted from his apartment. He had no one to come and pick up his items, so I had Bernard bring a truck so that we could get his stuff out of the rain. It has been fourteen years since I'd met Bernard, and we have raised our daughter together with very little problems. Whenever I have asked him to be there, he has been for the girls, my brothers and me. Bernard is *family* and one of the only people I truly trust. It didn't surprise me that he was there to help my brother.

Perry has had financial problems since our mother died six years ago. He was the one that didn't want to sue Crawford Long Hospital for the premature death of our mother, but as we sat in the rain, he mentioned to me that he would have done it now if he could. I told my brother that now he would have been doing it for the wrong reasons.

I remember my mother's funeral. It was the last time I'd ever wore a dress. I wanted to say that back in Chapter 13, but was too choked up to type anymore. Perry was always ashamed that his little sister was a butch lesbian. He never had the guts to tell me to my face. He bought my mother a royal blue suit to wear when she died. It was beautiful! I know she was pissed off that he waited until she was dead to buy her that! He also bought him and my other brother a suit to match her royal blue. He bought me nothing. The day of my mother's funeral I went through her closet, I found one of her dresses, and I wore it with one of her favorite dress hats and a pair of her heels. Not because anyone told me to—but because I wanted to! I did it for her.

When I got to my brother's house, they didn't even recognize me. I had worn shirt, tie, and slacks for so long. However, I swore that in honor of my mother that I would wear her dress and that would be it. My brothers didn't leave room for my daughters or me in the first limo behind my mother's hearse. We rode in the second limo. My daughters, Bernard and myself. Everyone was so angry with Perry after the way he treated me that day. My cousins really lashed into him before they left.

I was ok. I never mentioned it to him, and never will. He still had saved my life years ago. I had to learn that just because he didn't understand me, didn't mean that deep down he didn't love me. When he needs me, I always will be there.

My brother nestled into another home and so did I. That is when I moved into these apartments with the lake in Lithonia. I was an untouchable wreck! I had ended my friendship with Gail, because it was necessary to forget her, as it was Lauralee. I can't be friends with ex-girlfriends or people that I have slept with. It cuts down a lot of confusion and drama. I definitely had no drama in my life, because I was very dead in the months following my thirty-sixth birthday. I was poor in appearance, and didn't really take care of myself as I should have. I had totally lost all interest.

In late August, I attend Black Gay Pride here in Atlanta. I also started a community website call FAMnation, which is for the Black and Latino gay community and admirers. It was something to do. It doesn't make any money. I just wanted to do something different. I was torn up at Black Gay Pride! I admit it. I had just accepted the truth about Lauralee, and just didn't give a hoot! I hoped for a pick me up this year, but all I got that weekend was lesson after lesson, and reminder after reminder.

I saw someone that I knew back in grade school. I had found out that he was gay at the Marquette a while back. I had known him for years and he could have been in a bunch of chapters in this book including the first few! Eldridge use to pick on him, too! The problem was that we grew into similar professions. We both worked with computers and had our own businesses. He never used my services, but I would patronize his every time I had a new idea.

One year, our businesses clashed with a conflict of interest from a person that was mutual friend. After the conflict, this person said that they had to make the choice on whether to keep me as a client, or as a friend. He chose to keep me as a client.

That hurt me beyond reason because we had known each other for years. I loved him at one time even more than my own brothers.

He spoke with me once, but as the weekend went on, I called out to him and he ignored me. All those years I used his services because he was my friend. I was wrong in doing that, and set myself up. I don't blame him at all. It was my fault.

Business is *business*, and friendship is something totally other than that! If I had learned that, then it would not have hurt me so much that he had made that choice.

The lessons kept coming. I was sitting on a bench outside the Sheraton hotel when this butch came up to me. She was from St. Louis and wanted to know where to buy some cigarette papers to roll some weed.

(Ok. I admit that I was looking quite rough then, and that I would look like a person that would know!)

I did tell her that the Southern thing to do was to use a Blunt cigar instead of the papers. I don't do the weed or the drug thing. However, I did point her in the right direction to buy a cigar. She offered me a drink of brandy instead.

She invited me up to her room and told me that she was leaving her girlfriend after this trip. She was in her mid-fifties and said that her girlfriend was tying her down. We talked for a few minutes while she smoked her weed and it was extremely strong! When we left to go downstairs, it was all on my clothes as if I'd been smoking!

The entire floor where they had a room was lit up like Jamaica nights! You could smell it all over the hotel when we walked. Fortunately, we weren't arrested, but this butch was something else! She had a way with people. She talked with just about everyone in the lobby.

We ran into a femme, and her femme friend, that I had met that worked for Southern Voice, and she asked the butch if she wanted to "hang with us", or "hang with JohnTre"?

What the hell?

I was really hurt and the brandy had started to work!

"Oh, so I'm not good enough to hang out with you?", I said. The Southern Voice woman just walked away without saying anything.

That was really cruel of her! I know I was messed up that day, but all I need was a little love—*and some coffee!*

The butch kept calling her girlfriend and asking her to bring back the rental car that she'd paid for. They were really going at it over the phone! I was drowning myself in sorrow and her brandy. It was obviously one of those times in your life that you wish you had a do-over!

However, I had a listening ear so I talked away to this butch about Nichelle, Lauralee, and Gail and even mentioned the sacred briefcase of all the women disasters I've had.

Her story could have almost *mirrored* mine! She had been out for over 30 years and had gone through the same rough times. But, she said that she knew when to get out of a relationship, and that was one of the things I had to learn. I also had to remember not to get into ones that I didn't want, and to not mislead, or to be misled into anything.

I didn't look at her as a mentor because it was hard to while she was rolling a blunt and I was drinking brandy! However, she did have a point about a few things.

We went downstairs and her girlfriend pulled up in the rental car with her daughter. They had been shopping and had used the butch's credit card to the limit! It was a huge argument between them and in the midst, since I was going to be their

Atlanta tour guide, I asked the butch to introduce me to them. The girlfriend's daughter from H.E.L.L. responded,

"Oh, no introduction is necessary!"

She then took the bags of newly purchased clothes and went up to their hotel room.

After "meeting" the daughter, I wanted to leave, but I had promised the butch that I would go out with her, and she drove me all the way to Lithonia to pick up my clothes in the rental. This was the first butch to ever act as if she wanted to be a friend, so I couldn't let her down.

I came home, made sure my daughters were ok, dropped off my bag and left! My daughters were happy that I had met a butch friend and not another girlfriend! I think my heartaches were beginning to make them weary of me bringing home new love interests.

We went back to the hotel and I finally met the girlfriend. She seemed ok, but reminded me of Tamela in looks and behavior. She and the butch had plans before she came and met me! She had wanted to go to the White Party and Jeans or something. Looks like my new butch friend was using me as an escape! I wasn't used to a butch doing that. Nope, I didn't like it. But, a promise was a promise!

It turned out that the girlfriend used to live in Atlanta a while back, and asked me about directions to the old Marquette location and other hot, gay nightspots that she remembered.

"You've been gone a while! The Marquette has moved but it is still open", I said. Then I had to break the news to her that there was no more Texas, Lorettas, (technically speaking—it was another gay club now), Backstreet, or the Otherside".

(We'll take a moment of silence for Backstreet, here.)

The two started arguing about going out and the daughter from H.E.L.L. jumped in. She promptly evicted me from the room as they were having a family argument that as she put it, "didn't concern me." I saw this as the moment when I should leave when the butch stopped me in the hallway.

"Hey L.A., don't leave! I can handle them! You've had a rough year like me, and we are going out to chill, ok! Forget these broads!"

By that time, the entire Sheraton ninth floor came out into the hall to see what the ruckus was! Everyone was *family*, as Black Gay Pride generally takes up the entire hotel that weekend. The butch and her girlfriend had also befriended a group of people across the hall that were now asking me what was going on with their new "St. Louis Family", as they put it.

They finally came into the hall, and my butch friend told me to come back in the room so that we could plan the night out. Apparently, she had gotten everything under control because they weren't arguing anymore.

The people in the hall were laughing and joking with the couple about up North, and asking them what were they doing that evening. I was standing by the butch because she had asked me to when one of the people across the hall with a camera starting yelling,

"Can I get a picture of my new St. Louis Family please?"

She repeated it several times. I was in the way of the photograph, and high from the brandy, so I didn't move, nor did I know what she meant.

I stepped out of the way briefly to see who was coming off the elevator when I heard, "Thank you, duh! Get a clue!", and the flash flickered behind my head.

What the hell, again?

"Oh, I'm sorry was I in the way?" I asked. None of them even said a word—not one freaking word!

Isn't that a crock of crap! They wanted to front because I wasn't good enough for the picture, but when I asked you if I was in the way, you can't say anything! Instead, you want to "duh" me!

I was tired of getting dissed, and tired of being so polite to people all these years that keep dogging me! I wasn't Black enough this year for the red haired lady, but I felt a rush of color in me right then! I was really getting boiled inside, and turning bright Cherokee red on the outside!

Then, the butch, as if she could read my mind, said "Hey, that's not you! Let it go. It's going to get better, trust me! It ain't easy being who we are! Our own folks'll dog us out just because we are down! But, you will rise again and I know it! Stay strong!"

The St. Louis family would argue again for the fifth time that evening, I would hear the daughter from H.E.L.L. say that she wasn't going to insult her anymore and stormed out the door.

She looked at me and called me a butch-ass bitch and left! I said something so fowl back in retaliation that I won't even type it here.

My butch friend heard me and yelled out again, "That isn't you! Stop doing that!"

(Well, stop giving me brandy then! It's truth serum!)

We didn't go to the Marquette and missed the party that they were supposed to go to as well. Actually, we wound up at a hetero bar of all places, and the bouncer let us in free! I hadn't been to a hetero bar in years, and seeing those couples again felt like I was on another planet. It seemed like I had been in a completely different country for the past thirteen years!

The butch bought me three drinks that night. I had money, but she would not let me spend it. Her girlfriend was extremely angry with her and threatened to walk to the Marquette. She was a good 20 miles away. I asked the butch what was really up with everything.

"She doesn't want me. She wants my money. Her daughter and all of them just want to use me. My card is almost over the limit. You see what being with these women that don't care will do to you? Is this what you want for yourself, L.A.?"

After another argument from them, we left the club. The girlfriend suggested that we try Lorettas because she wanted to be around gay people at least once tonight! I informed her that the club was still there—but was now called 708, that it was mostly gay men there tonight, and the cover charge was around $20 because of the holiday.

We had another femme with us that quickly said that she didn't have the cover. The girlfriend said that the butch would pay her way in because she was a *big baller*. That's not something that you say about your boo if you're in love with her. My butch friend was right.

We made it back to the hotel and my butch friend was plastered! My drinks were wearing off, and I helped the girlfriend pour the butch into her hotel bed. Well, that is after we actually got her off the hotel hallway floor! Poor buddy! She was drinking and smoking herself to take her mind off the fact that she was in another dead-end relationship in her mid-fifties. She wanted me there to pass on some wisdom, and to have some support.

"Well, thanks for the evening. I'm leaving now", I said and wrote my number for the girlfriend to give to the butch, who was almost fast asleep.

The girlfriend asked if I had a ride and I said yes, and I told her to thank the butch for everything, and I apologized for calling her daughter that fowl name when she left. *Even though she deserved it!*

I didn't have a ride, of course! I just walked down to the Five Points station and waited for the first train to take me back to Indian Creek near Lithonia.

I was shown something that evening. That butch showed me what my life would be like twenty years from now if I didn't stop dating women that I didn't want to be with and that used me.

I never got a phone call from the butch and I don't even remember her name, but she saw herself in me and wanted to stop me from making the same mistakes, and I'm grateful for that.

I was untouchable by femmes in those last few months of 2006! I just couldn't do it anymore! I was not going to end up like my butch friend from St. Louis and hurting in my fifties. I'd stay alone if I have too. I know that's ridiculous to say because finding the woman of my dreams is all I've ever wanted to be happy. I always wanted a family that understood me, and I could be who I was! Not Lisa, but L.A. JohnTre!

After Black Gay Pride, I started promoting FAMnation and got it up to about 500 members. I wasn't surprised that Lauralee and Gail both joined the site to start meeting new people. I was still in a rut, and didn't come out to meet many people. I kept my promise to say away from that chat line, but there was still the Internet!

Several femmes approached me from my Internet site and I avoided trying to start a relationship with any of them. I was now certain that I was destined to be a butch bachelor and it even says that in my profile. I didn't feel that I was going to meet a woman with all of the qualities that I desired and that liked butches. I was trying to condition myself to get used to that, but there was still one more lesson that I needed to learn!

"Jess"
Final Lesson?
(2006)

The woman that I was talking about when I started writing this book by the lake was Jess. I was on the internet one day and decided to go back to the lesbian site that I used be on frequently where I met Yolanda. I did a search and saw two women that I added to my favorites. I did another search for a younger woman and saw Jess!

Oh my God! I couldn't believe it! Not only was Jess beautiful, she loved butches, and didn't live far from me. She spoke fluent German and some Spanish. She was just gorgeous. I knew she wouldn't respond, but I went and paid the $15.00 for response time and sent her a message.

(I know! I did something stupid didn't I? I was back on the Internet looking for someone instead of waiting for her to find me! I know! I know! But, I just couldn't help it! Jess was just too irresistible to me! Her profile was perfect!)

I also answered the other two ads that I placed in my favorites. I had to laugh when I took a second look at one of them. She had on a leopard print suit in one of her photos. *Leopard?* I took a closer look and it was Miss Cartier! Remember her? It had been over eight years since I'd seen her! I wonder if she got that ring? I didn't recognize her, but I'm quite sure she knew it was me and didn't respond. That was a good thing.

I was sitting on my bed when my phone rang. I looked at the caller ID and it said "Jess"! I was so shocked! She called me back! *Yes!*

She had a glorious accent that just melted me. We broke into conversation and we really hit it off well. Here was a woman that had everything I could ever hope for in a mate. She was an artist and even sent me some of her work. She also had a great Myspace page and I would visit it frequently to see if she posted new poetry. I didn't want her to join FAMnation yet, but I told her about the site, so that she would know that it was my work.

Maybe I was a little too excited and wanted too much too fast with her, but if you've read all of this up until now, you'd know that I really wanted someone this special in my life! I was inspired to actually write poems for Jess. I hadn't done that in years! She said that she liked reading the poems that I sent her and wanted to meet me soon.

I sponsored the Clik Awards at the Fox Theatre this year and was debating on whether or not I would go. I had bought some extra tickets for a FAMnation member giveaway and the winners opted for an alternate prize. I wanted to take Jess with me so that she could meet some people in the industry. She had some great contacts already, but I knew that this would be a great opportunity for her. I asked her and she said that she would love to go! *Yes!*

We had decided to choose complementing colors to wear to that event and met a few days before for the first time at Stonecrest Mall. I got a bouquet of fresh cut flowers and met her at the Borders entrance. *Oh my!* She was astounding! I had never seen a more beautiful femme in all of my life! We met and embraced in the parking lot and I was sure that the Universe was going to turn all the tables. All of the ex-girlfriends, gold diggers and users would finally be erased from my memory. I would only think of Jess!

We ordered hot wings from the restaurant and Jess asked me if I was disappointed in her. *As if?* I was glowing from ear to ear. We leaned over to each other and exchanged some very good body vibes! This beautiful woman was really feeling me! It felt so good. She was much more than beautiful. I also enjoyed her way of looking at things! I told her when the wings got there that I eat messy and she laughed.

"Food should be fun!", she said. It was fun too! I had never enjoyed a plate of scorching hot wings before in such great company.

She took me to her house to meet two of her friends and co-workers. On the way, she hooked me on to German born singer Xavier Naidoo, and played one of his songs. When we got there, her co-workers were fun guys, and we laughed and sang songs that I hadn't heard in years!

This was great! I felt like the tides were turning for me. I felt like finally my world was in *balance*, and that was the Tarot card I pulled that day from my personal horoscope and reading.

It said that all the bad things that I had been going through would change for the better, to keep the "balance" in Karma!

Jess insisted that she meet Vee and Tee that evening. Her friends drove and I leaned over to her and kissed her in the back seat. She straddled my legs and I damn near heard the heavens open as she kissed me back passionately. The ride was so short because in no time, we were at my house and I had to let her go.

I had called the girls beforehand to let them know that we were coming to get them. Jess came into the house and I introduced them. They really liked her, too. We went bowling that night in Conyers and had to leave because Jess was getting extremely tired. She had gone well beyond the call of duty that night and left us, especially me, wanting more!

I woke up the next morning, which was Thanksgiving, to Jess's phone call. She said that she had a great time and couldn't wait to see me that weekend. She wished me and my daughters a Happy Thanksgiving. She was on the way to her parent's house, and would try to call me later that evening. I was so inspired that I wrote her a poem and the girls designed an e-card to show her how then enjoyed her that evening!

The next morning I waited for a phone call from Jess. I got an email instead. I had sent her my poem and was anxiously waiting to see what she thought of it. I eagerly opened her email to see what she had sent me.

Good morning...

Tell your girls that I thank them very much for their kind words. I feel very flattered that they would take the time to send me such an adorable email. They are sweet as pie. Thank you for your poetry also. That was beautiful as well as words..thank you much..

I hate to spoil the moment and all, but I'm afraid I have some bad news, I don't think I will be able to attend the award with you Saturday. I am so sick and even more I feel so bad that you have already bought the tickets and now approx 24 hours before the event I must back out. Please do understand that I want to accompany you, but I am really not well and I feel as though I have been gargling a hand full of nails. My throat hurts so badly that it was really unwise for me to go anywhere these past few days. I should have kept myself at home doped up and in bed. Last night I found myself with a high fever and have been taking 800 mg pain killers and I still feel it..on top of that my voice is slowly leaving me and I sound like ET's twin sister.

I understand if you wish not to speak with me anymore, or should you not care to see me again. That too I understand. I do apologize if I have cause any inconvenience.

Once more
My sincerest apologies
Jess

(I left this page blank for **"BALANCE"**)

That damn football! That damn Lucy!

I had a theory. I said the first night after I met her that if we made it to this event, then she was the **ONE**. I knew it! There was no doubt in my mind about it. I wanted to go with her so bad! I wanted this to happen so much and if it happened—then I would know!

To her credit, she *was* sick that day. She felt really horrible and was even sick that evening at the bowling alley. If she had just cancelled going to the event, then I would have had more hope, but did you catch it at the end? The "way out"?

I understand if you wish not to speak with me anymore, or should you not care to see me again. That too I understand. I do apologize if I have caused any inconvenience.

No! Not the way out! What happened that night after you left your parents? I will never know, but it was obviously something! Somebody said something, and I'm banking that it was the one who she was really in love with! She totally changed her attitude and those last lines said that you could contact me if you want to or not. I'll understand if you don't and will go on with my life and you do the same! No! Say it wasn't so!

I could've taken that "way out". But, I kept thinking about her precious lips and those kisses! I kept thinking about how sweet she was, and that beautiful voice, so I responded:

Hello Jess,

Just feel better ok? I'm going to get my suit today. I'm not like other people. I won't stop talking to you just because you had to cancel a date. The only way that I will stop talking to you or feel that you aren't interested is if you stop communicating with me. Will you draw me a picture or write me something while you are mending. If so, I would like that.

L.A.

I responded to a "way out"—with a "way out" for her! *Yeah, that was stupid, huh?* Plus, I was smitten by her so much that I had no idea of what to do. It would have been so much easier if she hadn't kissed me that day! That captivated my lonely ass like crazy and I couldn't think straight!

I had met another author from my FAMnation website, whom would be gracious enough to be my date for the awards show after Jess cancelled. She told me that she thought Jess was "bullshitting" me anyway. I told her that I thought that Jess was in love with someone that already had someone else, and that person had probably given her some daylight that evening.

"I don't know what to do! I really want this girl! She is so sweet, and she has a lot in common with the girls and me! I don't want to think that was just a one night thing!"

I would call and email Jess every day. She would stop responding to the romantic emails I sent and just focus on the business stuff I sent her. *(Lauralee déjà vu)* I told her that I would pass out her name around at the event, which I did. She would call me at times still, but our conversation was different from before. It was mostly me doing all of the talking and it would be hard to get Jess to respond. In fact, she was becoming much more defensive in our conversations.

I wasn't stupid. I knew what was happening. She told me to be patient, and that she was trying to get to know me. *(Tamela déjà vu).* You and I both know that is a bunch of crock! If a woman wants you—then she wants you! *She will go for you!* Jess had even written that she was the one that had walked up to her previous girlfriend and expressed interest in her! That sounds like a woman that goes and get what she wants and not one that has to wait around! *I'd love for a woman like that to come up to me!*

I was so disappointed knowing that Jess didn't actually want me, that I went down by the lake and just started writing. The ironic part is that because of Jess, I wasn't even thinking about Lauralee anymore! It's like I replaced old hurt with new hurt. That can't be healthy!

A few days went by and Jess called twice while I was at the grocery store. Tee had answered the phone and told me that Jess was really trying to get in touch with me. I put the food away and quickly called her.

"Can you get a babysitter for tonight?", she asked. Her voice was back to that way I remembered when we had first met. She was really sweet and irresistible again.

"My girls are big girls. They don't need a babysitter. Why what is wrong?"

She told me that she just wanted my company and to be there at 9:00PM. It was already passed the hour and I told her that I may have to catch the bus and she pick me up from the station. Jess told me that she had been drinking and didn't want to drive. I admired her for that! My car has serious transmission problems, and I didn't know if it could make it to her house.

I had a decision to make. This was a beautiful, artistic, bilingual femme that is interested in butch lesbians! She's the epitome of the woman that I've been searching for all my life! She's been a little rude to me in the past few days and deep down I know she's been wanting someone else, but maybe she's changed her mind and wants me now. I would have to be crazy not to give take chance!

I got into my Ford Taurus station wagon and talked to *her*. I always talk to and name my cars. I told my car that I had to get down the road and that we weren't taking the freeway! I stopped midway and filled up the car with gas. I then took a few shortcuts avoiding police and cruised through Decatur to make it to her house. My car only went about 40MPH and had a faulty tail light. I certainly didn't want to be pulled over! I actually arrived with two minutes to spare and showed her my watch. She was impressed at my punctuality. I thanked my car for getting me there.

Only her Christmas tree lighted her apartment and she had German music playing as I entered. It was the most romantic setting that I had ever walked into! I was in paradise. Jess had been drinking, but she wasn't as stoned as that woman I had the date with in East Atlanta earlier this year, thank goodness! She was just really in a mellow mood.

She straddled me on her couch and I closed my eyes as I felt her. I had wanted to feel her before I actually saw her naked. She must've thought that it had been eons since I made love to someone the way I was carrying on! It had only been two months, but it was just that this time I was actually with someone that I wanted to be with!

After we left the living room, Jess told me that I was behaving too much and should show her how much I wanted her. *I thought I was!* When we were on her bed, I got to see how beautiful her body really was. I had it known it would be and I kissed every inch of it! It was enjoying her, but I don't think she was enjoying me. She made a request that I was hoping she wouldn't!

"Bite me. Show me how much you want to be with me!", she said.

Oh no! She was into that! *(London Déjà vu)* I'm a love maker and I do is very gentle. It would be why some woman would say that I'm a great lover, but some of the others would not like to be with me because they like it rough! To me that is abuse, even if the woman likes it. Jess was too beautiful for me to abuse. I still massaged her and loved her into a sleep, and I rested on the pillow next to her.

I didn't sleep that night. For one, I snore and didn't want her to hear me! But, the real reason was that I didn't want to miss her! Jess was lying there naked, with her smooth and creamy vanilla skinned body.

She had that beautiful long, black hair that waves up when she gets out of the shower and looks wet all day. Her hair rested on my arm as she murmured phrases in her sleep.

It wasn't English, she also speaks German and Spanish, so I guess it was one of the two! I just watched her for hours and kissed her gently every few minutes. Something just told me to savor every moment. I had been shown that a beautiful femme can desire a butch's company.

The next morning I relaxed her again. She had to get up and leave, but before she left my arms, I had to ask her to be my girlfriend. I knew that when a woman like her says that she wants to be with someone, then she is true to them. I totally wanted her and would have given all of me to make her happy. She was lighting a cigarette and almost burned herself. She said later that I shocked her when I asked!

"I don't even know you. It's only been about two weeks. It's too soon for that. It was too soon for us to do what we just did also, but it happened."

I wasn't surprised too much. "Do you regret that we've done this now?"

She said that she didn't have any regrets. I wasn't sure of exactly how I felt about it. I came there that night wanting to leave as Jess's butch companion. I didn't come just for the sex.

Maybe it was Karma for those other woman that I should not have dated. I had even told Rose a while back that I thought I was being punished for hurting her. She told me that she never wished that anything bad would happen to me and always prayed that I would find someone. Rose actually found her someone special and was partnered with her while I was with Gail.

Jess gave me a hug and told me thanks for coming over. We got into our cars and just left. What was that? Was I just a booty call?

I logged on to Jess's MySpace page the next day. Whenever someone as artistic as Jess has a great night, they usually write about it. I wrote a few poems for her after that evening and emailed them to her. She said that she never got them.

She didn't write an entry in her MySpace page about her night with me at all. It would have been like a *New York Times* review, or something. I didn't make the cut, or even an honorable mention. That sucks!

I had also asked Jess if she and her friends wanted to go to mountains next year for a trip. Once again, she said she didn't know me well enough for that. I told her that I wanted to become a part of her "family" and that I enjoyed hanging with her and one of her male co-workers that I'd met.

She said that she, the male co-worker and another butch were all the "family" that she needed, and that they were not "accepting applications" for new members. *Ouch.* That hurt, and was very disappointing, because I really liked the male co-worker friend, too. I had never met the butch friend.

I was on FAMnation shortly after that trying to set up some modules and saw Jess's pictures. She had joined the site and was already getting some hits from other butches. She didn't send me a message or anything to say hello, or let me know that she had joined. I called Jess and asked when she joined.

"It was just something to do. I had already met some people on there from Yahoo at one time, and wanted to get back in touch with them."

I saw what she had put in a message. She was really interested in meeting one of the site members. I thought back to the site where I saw her ad. My ad was still on there when she joined. If Jess really wanted to talk to me, then she would have sent me an icebreaker from that site.

Jess was the type of femme that will go after whom she wants, and she didn't approach me. She approached that person on Yahoo and FAMnation, and her ex-girlfriend, because she *wanted* them.

Jess told me that she thought I was rushing her into a decision about me, and it had only been three weeks since we met. She also apologized if she had mislead me into thinking that she wanted more with me at that moment. I asked her if she wanted me to "slow down" and she said yes.

"Why didn't just tell me that you wanted me to slow down, Jess?" I asked.

She told me that she had just "thought about it" when I asked her just then! Oh man, she had to think of stuff to say to me. She said that she would call me back that evening after she left work but she never did.

I checked my email the next morning and got a message from her through FAMnation. The message was simple and just said, "L.A. would you delete my account, or show me how to do it?"

It was just as if she was any other member asking me to do it. She didn't send me a personal email, or anything saying that she was sorry that couldn't call me back that evening. I tried to call her and it went to her voice mail, which she had changed the message.

On her voice mail was a romantic poem! Women do that when they want someone to hear that they were thinking about them. I tried to call again, but once again, she let it go to her voice mail.

I checked Jess's MySpace page after that and there it was—just as I had expected! She had put in not one, but two romantic poems that morning! (One mood was "happy", and the other was "horny". Nuff said!)

It was crystal clear! Whomever she was with that night, got the *review* that I was hoping I'd get! She was saying the hell with me, FAMnation, and everyone else! I knew then that it was enough. I sent her the email showing her how to cancel her FAMnation account. I then told her that I was off to finish writing my book, and ended the email, "Peace and Love my Dear Jess".

I wasn't mad at her at all! I am a fan of true love. Jess wanted someone else, and she wanted me to leave on my own. I can't fault her for that, and I hope she is happy with the person she chose. I never contacted her again. It's been over four weeks to the writing.

I pulled out my phone jacks and haven't received any phone calls and I have over 4,000 emails jammed in my Inbox that I will delete. If Jess even tried to contact me after that, then I will never know.

Sometimes it's best to KNOW without actually KNOWING! I don't think she ever email or called back, but she might have. Maybe she even changed her mind and decided that she wanted me instead, and kept trying to contact me but I wouldn't answer the phone! Yeah, right!

Maybe I will hit the lottery and win a million dollars, too! Either way, I'll never know because I haven't answered my phones, checked my emails, or bought a lottery ticket!

It heals better sometimes **NOT** to know.

December 27, 2006
7:20 AM
Lithonia, GA USA
(Location: by the lake)

So What Now?

Yes, it's really cold out here again! Well, I am back where I started twenty-five days ago. I'm sitting by this cold lake in Lithonia. Christmas went ok. My daughters loved their gifts, and so did Bernard and his new girlfriend. She isn't a new girlfriend, but I feel great that he finally decided to share that she does exist to me. I'd known about her for six years. I love him like a brother, and I'll always have his back! What a good man to stand by his "baby's momma" all these years, even if she is a butch lesbian!

(By the way, for Christmas I got one of those countertop griddles I'd always wanted!)

I checked online and found out that my father, Nathaniel, passed away in 2002. He never got to meet his granddaughters. Hopefully, one day I will go to Macon and search for some of his side of the family. They would really love to meet my daughters.

I've learned a lot being a man with a womb! We take care of our children and some of us spend a lifetime searching for that femme to compliment us. As you read, I spent the first part of my life covering up who I was to please everyone else. I lied to myself for many years and even tried a heterosexual marriage. You just will never be happy until you are true to yourself.

After I came out, I was brought into the lives of people who were searching for the same thing that I was. True love. Either I've been so in love with them or they were so in love with me! I've never found a femme that we could put both of them together.

I've never even been in a true butch-femme relationship, either. Gail is a stud now. She is even on FAMnation as a stud! She was my longest lesbian relationship to date.

Where is that true femme that we can make each other happy? I meet a woman that comes over as a true femme and she's an alcoholic and kicks me out of her house! I meet the woman of my dreams a month ago and she isn't feeling me because she's in love with someone else. I meet a woman with children that I wanted to be with, and would cherish her and them as I do my own! But, I'm not what she desires, or as she put it— I'm not "perfect for her" and that's what she is looking for!

Am I still looking? The answer is yes and no. I think that this last episode with Jess was to let me learn that there *are* women out there that have all the qualities and beauty that I want in a femme and that they do like butches as well! Jess wasn't for me, but she was for that person that she adores!

I would love a woman to adore me like that and that's what I am waiting for. Sometimes that femme has to come to you and make the first move. I think that is the case with me, so I'll just wait until she does! Then, I can be her Prince Charming and we can have a fairytale romance and live happily...*(well you know!)*

Just in case you are wondering how I feel since I've finally written all of this down. I'm still lonely and pissed off at the world! But, thank you so much for asking! No, not really. I'm actually quite calm and at peace. Will my life stay at peace once I sink a copy of this book into this freezing lake?

I honestly don't know, but I'm very optimistic that it couldn't get any worse than it already has! Just kidding! It's going to be great—I just know it!

Happy New Year 2007 and beyond!
Peace & Love Always.

-- L.A. JohnTre

January 1, 2010
1:21 AM
Lithonia, GA USA
(My home in Marbut Farms, Lithonia, GA)

It has been **three years** since I wrote the pages that you were reading. It's now New Years day, 2010, and I'm in my office at my new home in Lithonia. So much has happened that even when I read the pages in this book again, I was amazed.

First, the obvious thing happened. I changed my name yet again. I did it because I found myself in the years since writing these pages. I am no longer distressed, or unhappily trying to find the one person that will make my life better. I found them. It was finding faith in the Lord that I truly needed. I have been single ever since Jess in 2006. I have kept my mind focused on my goals for my daughters and myself. I am free.

My new name is L. Johnverrell.

I am living my dream as a writer, director and producer of films. You can even find a list of my works on the Internet Movie Database, (IMDB). I shot my first full feature movie, Het-Q, in January 2009. It is a film about men and women that appear as being gay or lesbian, but are really they are heterosexual. I wrote this film because I don't like the term, "metrosexual". I think a term like "heterosexually queer" makes more sense.

But, I can write another book about that altogether. What some of you have asked me to write about in emails is what happened to the people I mentioned in the book. What happened to Bernard? Others?

Well, Bernard and I no longer friends, and that brotherly love I had for him has vanished. He stopped helping me raise our daughter and caused me to finally have to take legal action against him. It surprised me too, trust me. I never thought I'd have to do that, but people change over the years. That's one of the lessons I had to learn.

In 2009, I also lost my oldest brother, Perry to tuberculosis. A number of events happened that helped us grow closer together until his death. We worked together on the same job, and I officially came out to him. He was not as judgmental as I'd expected. We had a great conversation.

You can recall how hurt I was after my mother's funeral that he left me out of everything and I felt like he didn't love me. We'll, as the Lord would have it, when he died, I had to pay for his burial plot. I drove his car behind the hearse that carried his casket. He didn't have nearly the lavish ceremony that he gave my mother. But, he was buried with the best that me and Tim could afford. I glad that I have another angel in heaven watching over me and my daughters.

A lot of you have said that you were touched by my story and understand how family and desire to be loved can take a toll on you. I read those pages again and couldn't believe how far I've come. I thank the Lord that I am so much stronger than I was then. I don't have to be in a relationship to be happy anymore.

I haven't given up totally on finding the right person for me. But, I admit it hasn't been a priority for several years now and I'm learning to live with being single and getting things done. Remember when I said pain used to help me finish things? Well, in these few years, I've found a more positive way. I've found the love of the Lord in me, and the greatest love of all. I actually love myself enough not to settle for anything less than what I deserve.

Happy New Year 2010 and beyond!
Peace and love always,
L. Johnverrell

MAN WITH
A WOMB

Thank you for purchasing. I welcome your feedback.

To contact the author:
ljohnverrell@almostbullet.com

Man With A Womb

L.A. JohnTre